MUSLIMS IN INDIA

MUSLIMS IN INDIA

ABUL HASAN
ALI NADWI

CLARITAS
BOOKS

1 2 3 4 5 6 7 8 9 10

CLARITAS BOOKS

Bernard Street, Swansea, United Kingdom
Milpitas, California, United States

© CLARITAS BOOKS 2019

This book is in copyright. Subject to statutory exception and to the provisions of relevant collective licensing agreements, no reproduction of any part may take place without the written permission of
Claritas Books.

First Published in April 2019

Typeset in Minion Pro 14/11

Muslims in India
By Abul Hasan Ali Nadwi
Translated by Mohamed Asif Kidwai

A CIP catalogue record for this book is available from the British Library

ISBN: 978-1-905837-53-3

Contents

INTRODUCTION	13
CHAPTER 1: The Influence Of Muslims On Indian Civilisation	19
Muslim Saints and Preachers	19
Rulers and Conquerors	19
Permanent Settlement and Spirit of Service	20
The Cultural Isolation of India	20
Contact with the Outside World	21
The Concept of Divine Unity	21
Equality and Brotherhood	22
Rights of Women and Other Social Reforms	23
The Writing of History	24
New Techniques	25
The Cultural Revolution	25
Babar's Account	26
The Cultivation of Fruit	27
Agriculture, Trade and Industry	27
The Reforms of Akbar and Sher Shah	28
Public Services	29
A Cleaner and Better Mode of Living	29
Medicine	30

Ten Gifts of the Muslims	31
Material and Spiritual Achievements	32
A Luminous Torch	32

CHAPTER 2: Muslim Scholars And Their Achievements — 35

Dual Responsibility	35
The Literary Endeavours of Indian Ulema	35
Works of International Repute	36
Prodigiousness	41
The Greatest Bibliography	42
Modern Writers	42
Hadith Scholars	43
Some Unique Contributions	44
Islamic Literature in English	46
Hindi	46
Arabic Language and Literature	47
Arabic Journalism	44
Present-day Writers in Arabic	48

CHAPTER 3: Some Outstanding Muslim Personalities — 51

Intrinsic Strength	51
The Exodus of Muslims Following Tartar Invasion	51
Great Monarchs	53
Statesmen	57
One Solitary Exception	59
Reform and Renovation	60

CHAPTER 4: Sufi Saints Of India And Their Impact On Society — 65

Sufi Orders	65
Popular Enthusiasm	66
Social Significance	68
Fearlessness	71
Propagation of Knowledge and Learning	73

Benevolence	74
Resignation and Contentment	76
Refuge of Humanity	78

CHAPTER 5: Indo-Islamic Culture — 81

Two Determining Factors	81
Characteristics of Abrahamic Civilisation	82
The Place of God in The life of a Muslim	82
Monotheism	85
Human Dignity and Equality	86
Lesser Attributes	86
Fine Arts	87
Islamic Morality	87
Indian Influences	88

CHAPTER 6: Some Special Features Of The Medieval Educational System — 91

Sincerity and Self-Denial	91
Devotion to Work	94
Devotion to Pupils	94
Attachment of Student to Teachers	95
Patronage by Kings and Noblemen	96
Concern for Spiritual Advancement	98

CHAPTER 7: Modern Religious, Cultural And Educational Centre Of Muslims — 103

Darul Uloom, Deoband	103
Mazahir Uloom, Saharanpur	105
Other Madrasahs of the Nizamiyyah Pattern	106
Darul Uloom Nadwatul Ulema, Lucknow	107
Madrasah al Islah, Sarai Mir	110
Darul Uloom Bhopal	110
Modern Institutions	110

Muslim University, Aligarh	111
Jami'a Millia, Delhi	112
Jami'a Osmania, Hyderabad	113
Intermediate and Degree Colleges.	113
Darul Musannifin, Azamgarh	113
Nadwatul Musannifin, Delhi	114
Majlis-i-Tahqiqat-o-Nashriyat-i-Islam, Lucknow	114
Muslim Educational Conference, Aligarh	114
Dini Talimi Board & Dini Talimi Council	115
Dairatul Ma'arif, Hyderabad	115
Darul Tarjuma (now defunct), Hyderabad	116
Jami'at-i-Islami's Institution at Rampur	117
Old Libraries	117
CHAPTER 8: The Role Of Muslims In The Struggle For Freedom	**119**
Muslims at the Forefront	119
Tipu Sultan's Crusade	119
The War of Independence	120
Muslim Leadership during the War of Independence	121
The Vengeance of the British	121
Death and Desolation	121
An Islamic Rebellion	123
The Mass Execution of Muslims	123
The Price of the Struggle for Freedom	124
The Exclusion of Muslims from Public Services	125
Unconcealed Vindictiveness	126
The Formation of the Indian National Congress	128
Sir Syed Ahmed Khan's Disagreement	128
The Support of the Ulema for the Congress	128
The Balkan war and its Repercussions in India	129
Maulana Mohamed Hassan of Deoband	129
Maulana Abdul Bari of Firangi Mahal	130
The Rowlatt Report	130

The Khilafat Agitation and Hindu-Muslim Unity	130
The Non - Cooperation Movement	131
British Atrocities on Moplahs	131
The Last Resort	132
The Shuddhi, Sangathan and Tabligh Movements	132
Countrywide Communal Conflagration	133
The Parting of Ways	133
The Separate Muslim Front and the Demand for Partition	134
Maulana Husain Ahmad and the Jamiat Ulema-i-Hind	134
Maulana Azad	135
CHAPTER 9: Current Difficulties And Problems	137
Trials and Hardships: A Necessity	137
Hindrances to Religious Preaching and Propagation	138
An Unjust and Partial System of Education	140
The Question of Urdu	143
The Economic Problem	149
APPENDIX	153
TABLE I: The distribution of the Muslim population of India according to State, as recorded in the 1971 Census.	154
TABLE II: Distribution of the Muslim population according to District.	156
TABLE III: Percentage increase and decrease of Muslims according to State during the decade 1961-71	158
INDEX	161
NOTES	171

Introduction

For the different nations and communities of the world to live together in peace, harmony and goodwill, and to maintain a state of peaceful co-existence, it is necessary not merely to gain an understanding of each other's characteristics, ideologies, heritages and historical achievements, but also to appreciate them and hold them as precious and worthy of preservation.

For this reason, it is necessary everywhere to acquire a proper knowledge of the language and literature, culture and civilisation, history and even fine arts of other peoples. One country sends a mission, comprising people of culture and learning, to another to study the prevalent psychological, literary and cultural patterns and to teach them some of their own. Institutions are set up and funded globally with the aim of promoting cultural ties and understanding with rest of the world. For this same reason, the Government of India has established a large organisation called the Indian Council for Cultural Relations, and there are also in operation here in our country several other private and semi-official bodies, like the Indo-Arab and the Indo-Iranian Societies. These strive through various means to foster and strengthen cultural ties with the peoples of other lands.

There is a general desire all over the world, including in our own country, to forge intimate contacts with far-flung lands at personal, intellectual and cultural levels – national self-interest calls for this, as does the issue of world peace.

Given this, is it not also necessary within our one country for those who are aware of our past intellectual and cultural attainments to teach the millions of others that have been living side by side with us for centuries in order to help shape our country's destiny? In fact, it is one of the curious contradictions of Indian national existence that one important section of the population is almost totally in the dark about the ancient heritage and background of the other important section. It has no knowledge of any basic facts about it. It does not appreciate the part it has played in the progress and development of our Motherland and in its recent struggle for freedom. It does not know its contribution to the country's complex evolution up to the present day, nor its desires and ambitions, nor its needs and difficulties in the existing national setup. This ignorance, despite the two communities having lived together for hundreds of years and sharing the various daily activities, is a serious shortcoming which should be removed without delay. Unity, trust and harmony among the diverse elements that go to make up the Indian population, which are a prerequisite for national integration and progress, cannot be produced whilst we remain unaware of each other's spiritual and emotional make-up, historical and social backgrounds and the possibilities we each hold for the future.

This tragedy, however, is not confined only to ignorance. Even more disconcerting is that a powerful tendency to obscure the history and culture of an entire community – its past achievements and the glorious contribution it made to the national fight for independence – has been established in our country. There

Introduction

is an ongoing campaign to present the Muslim era in India as an age of foreign, imperialistic domination, devoid of all virtue and greatness and failing to produce a single noteworthy personality or remarkable cultural or academic achievement. Nor does it acknowledge any single act of selfless service to the country's welfare and development, of which the nation could be proud, during the long battle for freedom against the British; the role of the Muslims has been cast as nothing more than that of a disinterested spectator, or if they did accidentally take part, nothing they did is deemed worthy of attention. By acting in this manner we are thoughtlessly depriving the lofty, evergreen tree of India of a rich fruit-bearing branch and asserting to the world that, for about a thousand years, this mighty tree remained barren and utterly unproductive, as if the season of autumn reigned supreme all over the country. This is entirely in opposition to what history tells us, not to mention casting a sad reflection on the innate human richness of our land. In this way, we not only perpetrate a cruel injustice on a community which dwells in our midst in its millions, but also cease to be fair and honest to the Motherland and to its past and future generations, so much in need of those role models provided by the illustrious figures from that period of their history. Furthermore, we can introduce India more effectively to the Islamic countries, whose friendship we wish to cultivate, by highlighting the memorable achievements of the Muslim period, and hence win recognition for it and its glory from their educated and enlightened circles. Given that the people of those lands are already somewhat familiar with the main personalities and achievements of that span of Indian history, such an endeavour is unlikely to present any great difficulty.

The realisation of this reality and need is the incentive for the writing of these pages. For one reason or another, it is not possible these days, whether for Muslims or non-Muslims, to read voluminous works in Persian or classical Urdu to enquire into the diverse cultural, literary, material and political achievements of that period of our history. What are needed, therefore, are brief, easy-to-read books which present glimpses of the history and way of life of that era, and thus serve as an introduction. In 1951, on my return from an extensive tour of the Middle East, I was invited by the All India Radio to broadcast a series of talks in Arabic on Indian Muslims. These talks were received favourably by some of the Indian missions, and they suggested their publication in the form of a booklet. The All India Radio also broadcast them subsequently in a number of other languages, and the International Arabic journal *Al-Muslimun*, based in Damascus, was kind enough to publish them in a number of instalments. Encouraged by this response, I felt that, if the talks were rewritten as essays and a few more papers on suitable topics added, the resulting volume could usefully serve the purpose I have just indicated. This volume was subsequently produced in Arabic. I am happy to say that the book was later translated into easy, fluent Urdu by my friend and colleague Syed Mahmudul Hasan Nadwi, the manuscript being revised by me and several improvements made. The Chapter "The Role of Muslims in the Struggle for Freedom" has been translated by my nephew, Mohammed el-Hassani.

In the present compilation, five new papers have been included which were not broadcast over the radio. These are:

(I) The Influence of Muslims on Indian Civilisation
(II) The Role of Muslims in the Struggle for Freedom
(III) Indo-Islamic Culture
(IV) Sufi-Saints of India and their Impact on Society
(V) Current Difficulties and Problems.

It is hoped that this book, with these additions, will be read with interest among the educated circles of the various communities that go to make up our people and prove of some value in reducing the ignorance and indifference that exists towards Mus-

Introduction

lims. It may also be helpful in promoting the tolerant, accurate national perspective that the country so badly needs today.

It is also hoped that many educated Muslims too will find in these pages something which will be new to them, will add to their knowledge about themselves, and go some way towards ridding them of the unjustified inferiority complex that has developed within them of late. The Muslims are not only citizens of equal status with everyone else in India, they are among its chief builders and architects, and they hold a position second to none among the peoples of the world for selfless service to the Motherland. They gave to India and the Indian Civilisation a new life and a new dimension, and they awakened its people to a new set of moral and spiritual values. Every patch of its land and every particle of its soil bears the imprint of their greatness and is a monument to their industry, earnestness and creative genius. In every aspect of Indian life and civilisation can be seen evidence of their noble aestheticism and cultural richness.

ABUL HASAN ALI NADWI
Nadwatul Ulama
November 21, 1960
Lucknow

Chapter 1

The Influence of Muslims on Indian Civilisation

Muslims Saints and Preachers

When they first came to India, many Muslims did so for purely religious motives and not for the sake of worldly gains. They brought with them the Islamic message of equity and social justice in order to show those suffering from oppression and seeking guidance a way to free themselves from their bonds and to benefit from the endless natural bounties offered by God's wide earth. The best examples of these dedicated, selfless preachers are those devoted followers of Islam under whose benign shadow thousands of oppressed Indians not only found shelter but also began to live as their own, beloved kinsmen. The names of Ali Hujwiri, Khwaja Moinuddin Ajmeri and Syed Ali Hamadani are noteworthy representatives of this group of holy men.

Rulers and Conquerors

Muslims also came as warriors, conquerors and upright rulers, notable individuals including Mahmud Ghazni, Muhammad Ghori and Zahiruddin Babur. These men of courage and ambition laid the foundations of a magnificent empire that continued to prosper for hundreds of years and carried the country to glorious heights of progress and prosperity.

Permanent Settlement and a Spirit of Service

In whatever capacity they came, Muslims always treated India as their home. Their belief was that the earth belongs to God and He places it under the supervision and safekeeping of whoever He wishes. They considered themselves to be the divinely appointed trustees of God's land and the servants of His people, and they took as their motto. "Every country is our country for it is the country of our Lord".

The Muslims therefore regarded India as their own country and their permanent residence. They willingly gave their best in its service, mentally, physically and spiritually, believing that the contribution to its development and prosperity would ultimately be to their own advantage; their own future and that of India being inseparably linked. This attitude of Muslim settlers towards India was radically different from that of the British and the other foreign imperialistic powers that were later, in whole or in part, to gain control over the land. These Western imperialists treated India like a cow to be milked as thoroughly as they could for the short period it remained under their control. The devotion with which the Muslims strove for the advancement and prosperity of India can only be understood in this context.

The Cultural Isolation of India

When Muslims first stepped on Indian soil, there already existed ancient sciences and philosophy and an abundance of food and raw materials. Culturally, however, India had long been isolated from the rest of the civilised world. The mighty mountains to the north and the sea on the other three sides had prevented it from having regular dialogue with the world beyond its borders. The last foreign invader to visit India before the Muslims was Alexander the Great. During the intervening period, India had remained almost entirely cut off from the outside world, with no exchange of knowledge between the two. No new ideas and no fresh cultural input had reached it from abroad. Nor had it been able to export any of its own ancient wisdom.

Contact with the Outside World

It was then that the Muslims made their debut onto the Indian stage. They were, at that time, the most advanced community in the East. They brought with them to India a new, practical and highly rationalistic religion, mature knowledge, a progressive culture and an evolved civilisation, that drew on the best that a number of nations had to offer. It represented a synthesis of the natural Arab disposition, the dainty refinement of the Persians, and the rugged simplicity of the Turks. In addition, they brought many other priceless gifts and virtues.

The Concept of Divine Unity

The most valuable of these gifts was the Islamic concept of divinity, which, in a single stroke, dispensed with all intermediaries between man and his Creator. There is absolutely no place in Islam for beliefs such as polytheism, the incarnation of God, or "the merging of man with the Almighty and becoming one with Him". Islam emphatically declares the sovereignty and absolute oneness of the Divine Being. He is One and Everlasting, He neither begets, nor is He begotten, and He has no partners in His divine acts; the creation, the sustenance, the management and the ownership of the Universe lie solely in His hands. It was entirely natural for a belief like this to have a powerful impact on the Indian mind, despite it having been out of touch for centuries with the pure monotheistic doctrine. Professor K. M. Panikkar states;

"One thing is clear. Islam had a profound effect on Hinduism during this period. Medieval theism is in some ways a reply to the attack of Islam; and the doctrines of medieval teachers by whatever names their gods are known are essentially theistic. It is the one supreme God that is the object of the devotee's adoration and it is to His grace that we are asked to look for redemption."[1]

Equality and Brotherhood

Socially, an immense change was brought about by the Islamic notion of human equality and brotherhood. Islam upheld no division of society into permanent classes, nor did there exist any community such as the Untouchables among the Muslims. Their belief was that no one was born unclean into the world nor were they predestined to be ignorant and excluded from gaining knowledge simply by the fact of their being born in a certain class. No trade or occupation was reserved for a particular section of humanity. Furthermore, they freely associated with each other at all levels, the rich strove with the poor in the pursuit of learning and there was freedom of profession for all. The concept of brotherhood, for the Indian mind and the Indian society, was something novel, which encouraged renewed thinking and did a lot of good for the country. The bonds of the existing class-ridden society were considerably relaxed and a withdrawal from the excessive rigidity of the caste-system was witnessed. The advent of Islam also acted as a challenge to social reformers in other fields. Pandit Jawaharlal Nehru offered the following comments on the uplifting influence of Islam and Muslims on the Indian social structure:

"The impact of the invaders from the north-west and of Islam on India had been considerable. It had pointed out and shown up the abuses that had crept into Hindu society—the petrifaction of caste, untouchability, exclusiveness carried to fantastic lengths. The idea of the brotherhood of Islam and of the theoretical equality of its adherents made a powerful appeal, especially to those in the Hindu fold who were denied any semblance of equal treatment."[2]

To quote another writer of repute:

"Islam's democratic challenge has perhaps never been equalled by any other religious or social system. Its advent on the Indian scene was marked by a profound stirring of consciousness. It modified the basis of Hindu social structure throughout northern India."[3]

Rights of Woman and Other Social Reforms

Another aspect is the recognition of the dignity that should be accorded to women and of their rights as respected members of the family and as life-partners of men. The significance of the rights bestowed by Islam on women, in a country where widows within noble families used to immolate themselves on the funeral pyres of their husbands, requires no elaboration. In the eyes of society, and even in their own eyes, they forfeited the right to live after the death of their husbands. The following lines from Bernier's travel account show the considerable efforts undertaken by the Muslims to suppress this custom of *suttee* from the earliest days of their rule.

"...the number of victims is less now than formerly; the *Mahometans*, by whom the country is governed, doing all in their power to suppress the barbarous custom. They do not, indeed, forbid it by a positive law, because it is a part of their policy to leave the idolatrous population, which is so much more numerous than their own, in the free exercise of its religion; but the practice is checked by indirect means. No woman can sacrifice herself without permission from the governor of the province in which she resides, and he never grants it until he shall have ascertained that she is not to be turned aside from her purpose: to accomplish this desirable end the governor reasons with the widow and makes her enticing promises; after which, if these methods fail, he sometimes sends her among his women, that the effect of their remonstrances may be tried. Notwithstanding these obstacles, the number of self-immolations is still very considerable, particularly in the territories of the *Rajas*, where no *Mahometan* governors are appointed."[4]

The Writing of History

The Muslims introduced several modern branches of learning into India, one of the most important of which was history. Until then, the writing of history was almost unknown in India, the only examples being religious treatises and a few epics, such as the *Ramayana* and *Mahabharata*. The Muslims produced a whole library of historical works that could favourably compare in authenticity and comprehensiveness with the endeavours made in this branch in any other country. A glance through Maulana Syed Abdul Hayy's monumental Arabic work *al-Thaqafah al-Islamiyyah fi al-Hind*[5] (Islamic Culture in India) shows what tremendous efforts were made by Muslims in the compilation of the history of India. To quote Dr Gustave Le Bon:

"There does not exist a history of ancient India. Their

books contain no historical data whatever, except for a few religious books in which historical information is buried under a heap of parables and folk-lore, and their buildings and other monuments also do nothing to fill the void for the oldest among them do not go beyond the third century B.C. To discover facts about India of the ancient times is as difficult a task as the discovery of the island of Atlantis, which, according to Plato, was destroyed due to the changes of the earth."

After admitting that the epics, the *Ramayana* and the *Mahabharata*, do shed some light on the prevalent conditions during those days, the writer goes on to add that, "The historical phase of India began with the Muslim invasion. Muslims were India's first historians."[6]

New Techniques
Liberality of the mind, originality of thought and new techniques of poetry and literature were taught to the Indians by the Muslims, and new insights and perspectives became possible as a result of the intellectual and literary integration that occurred. Muslims can also be credited with the birth of a new, beautiful, living and expanding language, which became the medium of communication and a vehicle of literary expression. I mean, of course, the language of Urdu, whose richness and elegance are beyond description.

The Cultural Revolution
The influence of the Muslims is most prominent in the spheres of culture, social manners and general mode of living. The Muslims revolutionised the pattern of life in the country and gave it a new form, entirely different from what previously existed, just as life

in modern Europe is totally unlike what prevailed there in the Middle Ages.

Babar's Account

In order to adequately appreciate the extent and value of Muslim influence on Indian culture, it is necessary to have some idea of India as it was before the arrival of Islam and the Muslims. Fortunately, Babar has left behind a vivid description of the cultural decadence that existed, enabling us to easily judge the Muslim contribution. However, it should be borne in mind that the Muslim impact on India began quite a long time before the coming of the Mughals. Babar writes in his memoirs, *Tuzuk-i-Babari*:

> "There are neither good horses in India, nor good flesh, grapes, melons, ice, cold water, baths, candle, candlestick or torch. In the place of the candle, they use the *divat*.[7] It rests on three legs: a small iron piece resembling the snout of a lamp is fixed to the top end of the one leg and a weak wick to that of another; the hollowed rind of a gourd is held in the right hand from which a thin stream of oil is poured through a narrow hole. Even in case of Rajas and Maharajas, the attendants stand holding the clumsy *divat* in their hands when they are in need of light in the night.
>
> There is no arrangement for running water in gardens and buildings. The buildings lack beauty, symmetry, ventilation and neatness. Commonly, the people walk barefooted with a narrow slip tied round the loins. Women wear a dress consisting of one piece of cloth, half of which is wrapped round the legs while the other half is thrown over the head."

Commenting on Babar's observations on the culture and backwardness of India, Jawaharlal Nehru states:

"Yet his accounts tell us of the cultural poverty that had descended on north India. Partly this was due to Timur's destruction, partly to the exodus of many learned men and artists and noted craftsmen to the south. But it was also due to the drying up of the creative genius of the Indian people. Babar says that there was no lack of skilled workers and artisans, but there was no ingenuity or skill in mechanical invention."[8]

The Cultivation of Fruit
Despite the fertility of its soil, few fruits were found in India and those too were of poor quality. Most of them were grown wild, with people taking little interest in the development of horticulture. By contrast, the Mughals possessed a refined palate and there was a great abundance of fruit in their native land. As a result, fruit cultivation progressed rapidly in India after their coming. Details can be found in the famous memoires of the Emperors Babar and Jahangir, *Tuzuk-i-Babri* and *Tuzuk-i-Jahangiri* respectively. The Mughals developed several new and delicious varieties of fruits as a result of extensive experimentation in grafting. The mango is a well-known Indian fruit, but before the arrival of the Mughals, only one variety, *Tukhmi*, existed. It was the Mughals who developed the beautiful, luscious, grafted mangoes, leading over the course of time to the introduction of numerous varieties of the fruit.

Agriculture, Trade and Industry
The case was the same with textiles. Dresses in India were generally made from rough, coarse cloth. A number of textile factories

were set up in Gujarat by Sultan Mahmud Shah, better known as Mahmud Baigrah (d. 1511), where cloth weaving, dyeing, printing and design-laying were undertaken. He also established industrial centres for stone and ivory carving and for paper-making. Gifted, as he was, with a creative mind, the Sultan succeeded in arousing a rare enthusiasm for advancing trade, industry and agriculture among his subjects. Maulana Syed Abdul Hayy states:

> "Among the Sultan's outstanding works in developing the country were the construction of mosques and schools and the planting of fruit-bearing trees and orchards. He inspired the people magnificently in these tasks. He also built wells and canals for irrigation. Skilled artisans and craftsmen came to him from Iran and Turkistan and set up their crafts and industries in his kingdom. As a result, Gujarat became a rich, fertile stretch of greenery, with flourishing gardens, dense groves and delicious fruit, as well as an important trading centre which exported cloth to foreign lands. This was due entirely to the ceaseless efforts of Sultan Mahmud and the keen interest he took in the welfare of his people."[9]

The Reforms of Akbar and Sher Shah

Cloth-weaving factories were also established during the reign of the great Mughal emperor Akbar. In addition, he introduced many valuable agrarian reforms pertaining to measuring land and assessing and collecting land revenue. Improvements were also made in the field of finance, especially in coinage and currency, both by Akbar and the earlier Mughal emperor Sher Shah. Sher Shah had a unique gift for legislation and administrative organisation, and in fact it was his example which Akbar later followed.

Public Services

Historical records such as *Tuzuk-i-Jehangiri* and *Ain-i-Akbar* offer detailed descriptions of the advancements made by Muslim rulers in different areas. They achieved great success in training animals and the improvement of livestock. They also built numerous hospitals, poorhouses, public parks and gardens, and tanks and canals. Maulana Syed Abdul Hayy, in his unique work *Jannat al-Mashriq*,[10] provides a long list of the hospitals and other benevolent public welfare institutions established and the development projects undertaken in India during the so-called Muslim Period.

All the huge highways that connect the western parts of the sub-continent with its eastern parts were constructed by Muslim kings and emperors. The most important of these is the one built by Sher Shah that runs for 3,000 miles (4,832 kilometres) from Nilab in Sind to Sonargaon[11] in what is now Bangladesh. After every two miles there was a caravanserai[12] with separate charitable food establishments for Hindu and Muslim travellers and a mosque. The Muezzin,[13] Imam[14] and Hafiz[15] for the mosque were appointed by the state. A pair of speedy horses were stationed at each caravanserai to carry the mail, so that letters and messages could be sent regularly from Nilab to the distant borders of Bengal. Fruit-bearing trees were planted on either side of the road whose fruit and shade were a great boon to travellers.

A Cleaner and Better Mode of Living

Above all, however, the Muslims acquainted the original inhabitants of India with a cleaner and better mode of living. They introduced culinary refinements and delicacies. They taught them the principles of hygiene and sanitation, the advantages of building airy houses and the use of cups and other vessels for food. Until then, even at large feasts, Indians used to eat their food from the leaves of trees, a custom still prevalent in some places today. In short, the Muslims brought about a significant change to Indian social customs, living habits, domestic comforts, and home-decoration. They ushered in a new style of architecture, distinct, in terms of its refinement, grace, symmetry and dignity, from all that preceded. The Taj Mahal is a notable example of the new type of Muslim Architecture. In the words of Jawaharlal Nehru:

"The coming of Islam and of a considerable number of people from outside, with different ways of living and thought, affected these beliefs and structure. A foreign conquest, with all its evils, has one advantage: it widens the mental horizon of the people and compels them to look out of their shells. They realise that the world is a much bigger and more variegated place than they had imagined. So the Afghan conquest had affected India and many changes had taken place. Even more so the Moghals, who were far more cultured and advanced in the ways of living than the Afghans, brought changes to India. In particular, they introduced the refinements for which Iran was famous."[16]

The same view was expressed by Dr Pattabhi Sitaramayya in his presidential address to the Fifty-fifth session of the Congress, held at Jaipur in 1948. He said that the Muslims had "enriched our culture, strengthened our administration, and brought near distant parts of the country... It (the Muslim era) touched deeply the social life and the literature of the land."

Medicine
The Muslims, moreover, brought to India a new system of Medicine, the Unani System, which before the dawn of modern medicine was universally recognised as the most advanced and scientific system for the treatment of diseases. In their heyday, the

countries of Iraq, Iran and Turkistan were the most important centres of the Unani system in the world, and it was there that its greatest exponents and practitioners were born during the medieval age. After the establishment of Muslim power in India, and encouraged by the generous patronage that Muslim rulers extended to men of learning and ability, a steady stream of outstanding masters of the system poured into the country for a period lasting over five hundred years. Due to the invaluable service rendered by these worthy men and their pupils, their dedication and skill, the Unani system reached its peak in India. In the face of this progress, the indigenous system of medicine faded into insignificance. No city or town was left without a practitioner of the Unani school. This system was cheap, simple and in harmony with the Indian climatic conditions. It thus spread quickly in India and brought great benefit to the population, composed as it was of the mainly poorer classes. Indeed, Indian physicians contributed further to its success. During the declining phase of Muslim rule, Delhi and Lucknow were its two major strongholds, and India now remains the only country where this system of medicine is still in vogue.

Ten Gifts of the Muslims

In a paper entitled *Islam in India*, the renowned historian Sir Jadunath Sircar enumerated ten gifts, which according to him, the Muslims conferred on India. Some of these we have already discussed in this chapter; the rest are as follows: (i) the establishment of contact with the outside world; (ii) political unity and uniformity of culture and dress, especially amongst the upper classes; (iii) a common official language and a simple style of prose, in whose development both Hindus and Muslims have participated; (iv) the promotion of regional languages under the aegis of the Central Government, so that general peace and contentment may ensue and equal opportunities for literary and cultural advancement may be made available to all; (v) the revival of maritime trade, originally practiced by the people of the south but which had long ceased; and (vi) the formation of the Indian navy.

Material and Spiritual Achievements
Speaking of the material and spiritual achievements of Muslims in India, W.W. Hunter, a noted anti-Muslim writer, has observed that:

> "The Musalmáns led several of these great land reclamation colonies to the southward, and have left their names in Eastern Bengal as the first dividers of the water from the land. The sportsman comes across their dykes, and metalled roads, and mosques, and tanks, and tombs, in the loneliest recesses of the jungle; and wherever they went, they spread their faith, partly by the sword, but chiefly by a bold appeal to the two great instincts of the popular heart. The Hindus had never admitted the amphibious population of the Delta within the pale of their community. The Muhammadans offered the plenary privileges of Islám to Bráhman and outcaste alike. 'Down on your knees, every one of you,' preached these fierce missionaries, 'before the Almighty, in whose sight all men are equal, all created beings as the dust of earth. There is no God but the one God, and His Messenger is Muhammad.' The battle-cry of the warrior became, as soon as the conquest was over, the text of the divine."[17]

A Luminous Torch
N.S. Mehta, a gifted Indian civil servant, says in the course of an article entitled *Islam and the Indian Civilisation*:

> "Islam had brought to India a luminous torch which

rescued humanity from darkness at a time when old civilisations were on the decline and lofty moral ideals had got reduced to empty intellectual concepts. As in other lands, so in India too, the conquests of Islam were more widespread in the world of thought than in the world of politics. Today, also, the Islamic world is a spiritual brotherhood which is held together by a community of faith in the Oneness of God and human equality. Unfortunately, the history of Islam in this country remained tied up for centuries with that of government with the result that a veil was cast over its true spirit, and its fruit and blessings were hidden from the popular eye."[18]

To sum up, as is evident from the preceding pages and the opinions we have examined, what the Muslims gave to India was far greater, more lasting and more valuable than what they took from it. The coming of Islam and the Muslims marked the beginning of a new era in India's history, an era of enlightenment, progress and prosperity, which can never be forgotten.

Chapter 2

Muslim Scholars and Their Achievements

Dual Responsibility
Muslims in India have always demonstrated their deep devotion and loyalty to the Motherland, giving their utmost for its material, cultural, intellectual and spiritual advancement. Yet at the same time they have remained steadfast in their attachment to their faith and to Islamic Civilisation. They have never become disconnected from the Muslim world, and time and time again they have been called upon to act as its leaders and torch-bearers.

It was, by no means, easy to integrate these two notably different homes: one spiritual and the other physical and political. Across the entire Islamic world, no other group of Muslims has been so successful in undertaking this dual responsibility.

The Literary Endeavours of Indian Ulema
In this chapter, we will cover the profound contribution made by Indian ulema to Islamic studies. Even a sketchy work like Hajji Khalifa's *Kashf al-Zunun* (which attempts the impossible task of encompassing the entire Islamic world) does not fail to laud

the achievements of Indian Muslim scholars. However, Maulana Syed Abdul Hayy's *al-Thaqafah al-Islamiyyah fi al-Hind*[19] gives a clearer picture of the place India occupies in the development of Islamic literature.

Works of International Repute
Here, however, we will only refer to works that have become famous beyond the frontiers of India, having also won the praise of Arab scholars.

- We will begin with the work of the outstanding 13th century traditionalist and lexicographer, Hasan ibn Muhammad al-Saghani Lahori, *al-'Ubab al-Zakhir wa al-Lubab al-Fakhir*, which is still regarded as one of the most reliable and authoritative reference works in the Arabic Language. Students of lexicography have continuously drawn on it ever since and have unanimously acknowledged the profound learning and scholarship of its author. Imam al-Suyuti said of him that he was "a foremost authority on the subject of lexicography". Imam al-Dhahabi described him as "an embodiment of learning and an ultimate authority on lexicography"; and al-Dumyati stated that he was "a master of lexicography, Islamic jurisprudence and the science of Hadith." His other book, *Mashariq al-Anwar*, on the Hadith of the Prophet was, for a long time, a prescribed textbook in the educational institutions of various Arab countries and is still popular in the Islamic world.

- Another famous Hadith work is *Kanz al-'Um-*

mal[20], written in the 16th century by Shaykh Ali ibn Husamuddin al-Muttaqi Burhanputi[21]. This is an edited version of Imam al-Suyuti's *Jam' al-Jawami'*[22] and is considered one of most beneficial books on Hadith for students, saving them the trouble of having to plod through thick volumes of source-books and bibliographies. Commenting on the book, a notable scholar of the Hejaz belonging to the same century, Shaykh Abdul Hasan al-Bakri al-Shafi'i, remarked that "the entire world of learning is indebted to Imam al-Suyuti, and the Imam himself is indebted to Shaykh Ali Muttaqi."

- Then there is Shaykh Tahir Pattani's[23] (d. 1578) *Majma' Bihar al-Anwar fi Ghara'ib al-Tanzil wa Lata'if al-Akhbar*. Regarding it, Maulana Abdul Hayy writes in *Nuzhat al-Khawatir*:

> "In this book, the author has explained the meaning of difficult words and expressions occurring in the Hadith literature and has noted down under each word or expression the different hadiths where they appear. It has, thus, become a sort of key for the six most authoritative books of Hadith.[24] It has been popular among scholars from the very beginning and is regarded as the last word on the subject. The author has done a great favour to all people of learning by writing it."

- Another of Shaykh Tahir Pattani's works, *Tadh-*

kirat al-Mawdu'at, on the subject of fabricated hadiths is also a highly successful work.

- In the field of Islamic jurisprudence, the reference work *al-Fatawa al-Hindiyyah*, commonly known as *Fatawa-e-Alamgiri*, commands great respect. In Muslim countries where the Hanafi school if followed in matters of jurisprudence, a great reliance is placed upon this book for the interpretation of laws. Maulana Syed Abdul Hayy states:

> "*Al-Fatawa al-Hindiyyah*, which is also known as *Fatawa-e-Alamgiri*, is a most valuable book because of the wide range of legal principles it covers, as well as for the simplicity of its style and the ease with which it solves highly intricate issues. In the countries of Arabia, Syria and Egypt, it is famous by the name of *al-Fatawa al-Hindiyyah*. It is contained in six thick volumes and arranged on the lines of the book *al-Hidayah*."

The book strictly confines itself to commonly known and accepted rulings, leaving aside unconventional opinions and hypothetical issues. Where a commonly accepted ruling is not available on an issue, the relevant unconventional opinions have simply been reproduced, word for word, along with the name of the narrators, with no comments on these being offered. During the earlier years of his reign, the emperor Aurangzeb assigned the task of compiling the work to Shaykh Nizamuddin Burhanpuri, who worked on it with a team of scholars of the Hanafi school. Over 200,000 rupees were spent on compiling it. Shaykh Nizamuddin

Burhanpuri mentions the names of twenty-four experienced research workers who assisted him in writing the book. Four of them were Qadi Muhammad Husayn Jaunpuri Muhtasib, Shaykh Ali Akbar Husayni Asadullah Khani, Shaykh Hamid ibn Abu Hamid Jaunpuri and Mufti Muhammad Akram Hanafi Lahori, who jointly supervised the compilation of the book.

- *Musallam al-Thubut fi Usul al-Fiqh* by Imam Muhibullah Bihari (d. 1707) forms an important title in this series of writings. It earned great popularity in the educational institutions and literary circles of India and the Islamic World. Commentaries on it were written by celebrated scholars, with ten such commentaries being mentioned in Maulana Abdul Hayy's *al-Thaqafat al-Islamiyyah*.

- Maulana Muhammad A'la Thanwi's *Kashshaf Istilahat al-Funun* is a most valuable dictionary of literary and technical terms. It was compiled in the 18th century and has been universally celebrated as a remarkable achievement. It was the first book of its kind in the Arabic language and is still in wide use today.

- This was followed shortly after by Maulana Abdun-Nabi Ahmednagri's *Jami' al-Ulum* (also known as *The Scholar's Compendium*), which runs into four volumes.

- We now come to a book of rare worth and quality: Shah Waliullah's (d. 1762) *Hujjatullah al-Balighah* on the nature and philosophy of the Islamic Shariah and the fundamental principles governing legislation in Islam. It is an absolutely unique work on the subject, the like of which does not exist in the entire corpus of Arabic literature. It has been lavishly praised by scholars and literary critics and has been reprinted in Egypt several times. Apart from the great merit of its contents, the book also stands out as an eminently successful piece of writing in Arabic, with a simple eloquence and a lucid style. The fashion in those days was to write in heavily embellished language after the manner of Hariri. Shah Waliullah broke with this tradition and employed language that was free, easy and fluent. After Ibn-Khaldun's *Prolegomena*, *Hujjatullah al-Balighah* offers the most noteworthy example of graceful, yet effortless prose during a period that saw Arab intellectual decline and a preference for the ostentatious and the picturesque in Persian literary expression.

- The giant lexicon, *Taj al-'Arus min Jawahir al-Qamus* by Syed Murtada Bilgrami (d. 1790) hardly stands in any need of introduction or praise. Spread over ten volumes and more than 5,000 pages in small type, this book is like a library in Arabic lexicography. It needed great courage for an Indian scholar to undertake the compilation of an Arabic lexicon of such comprehensiveness and magnitude, completing, revising and enlarging the authoritative Arabic dictionary, *al-Qamus al-Muhit*, by that pillar among lexicographers, Majduddin al-Fayruzabadi.[25] *Taj al-'Arus* acquired such renown during the lifetime of its compiler that the Ottoman Sultan and the rulers of Darfur[26] and Morocco had special copies of it made for them, and a copy was also acquired at a cost of 1,000 riyals by that great Egyptian warlord and scholarly chieftain, Muhammad Abu Dhahab, for the library of the mosque he had built near the University of al-Azhar.

Prodigiousness

In the nineteenth and twentieth centuries, also, India proudly boasts of having produced Islamic scholars who were, and are the envy of the whole Muslim world for the prodigiousness of their literary output. For instance, Nawab Siddiq Hasan Khan of Bhopal (d. 1889) had 222 books to his credit, of which 56 were in Arabic, including *Fath al-Bayan fi Tafsir al-Quran* (10 volumes), *Abjad al-'Ulum, al-Taj al-Makallal, al-Bulghah fi Usul al-Lughah* and *al-'Alam al-Khaffaq fi 'Ilm al-Ishtiqaq*.

The writings of Maulana Abdul Hayy of Firangi Mahal, Lucknow, (d. 1986) number 110. Of these, 86 are in the Arabic language, *al-Si'ayah fi Kashf ma fi Sharh al-Wiqayah*, *Misbah al-Duja*, *al-Ta'liq al-Mumajjad* and *Zafar al-Amani* being of outstanding merit. His *al-Fawa'id al-Bahiyyah* is considered to be the most reliable work on the lives and activities of the ulema of the Hanafi school, and whenever information is sought regarding them, it has become conventional to look here.

As for Maulana Ashraf Ali Thanwi, by the time of his death, he had produced as many as 910 books, 13 in Arabic.

Finally, Maulana Baqar ibn Murtaza Madrasi and Mufti Muhammad Abbas Lucknavi also deserve special mention among the later-day scholars for their prolificacy. Both of them have left behind a large number of books and pamphlets on various subjects in both Arabic and Persian.

The Greatest Bibliography
The bibliography, *Mu'jam al-Musannifin*, compiled by Maulana Muhammad Hasan Khan of Tonk (d. 1946) is a breathtaking work of industry and scholarship. It runs into 20,000 pages, is divided into 60 volumes and deals with 40,000 authors. As a proof of its astonishing thoroughness, it is enough to know that it lists some 2,000 authors under the name of Ahmad alone. In fact, this amazing bibliography covers all the Muslim scholars who wrote even a single book in Arabic from the beginning of Islam until 1931. Four volumes of it have so far been published in Beirut at the expense of the Government of Hyderabad (Deccan) – now defunct – while the manuscripts of the rest are perhaps preserved in the Asafia Library, Hyderabad.

Modern Writers
Maulana Syed Sulaiman Nadwi (d. 1953) holds pride of place among Islamic scholars of the present times for the admirable contributions he has made to literature, the study of the life of the Holy Prophet, Islamic law and history. His works cover more than 7,000 pages, not including the numerous articles, notes and reviews he wrote for the Classical Urdu literary journal *Ma'arif*, which, by themselves, run into hundreds of pages. Based on his formidable achievements in the literary world, Maulana Syed Sulaiman Nadwi was, without doubt, a great writer and a genuinely important scholar of the East.

Another scholar who cannot possibly be overlooked, for his encyclopaedic knowledge and fluency of pen, is Maulana Manazir Ahsan Gilani (d. 1955). *Al-Nabiy al-Khatim, Tadwin-e-Hadith, Musalmano ka Nizame Taleem-o-Tarbiat* are among his more important works.

Hadith Scholars

As famous as the Indian scholars have been for their services to theological learning as a whole, they are without parallel when it comes to the study of the Hadith of the Prophet and their arrangement, analysis and elucidation. Ever since the end of the initial phase of Islam, they have consistently stood out as pioneers in this field. The famous Egyptian scholar Rashid Rida acknowledged the splendid work done by Indian Hadith scholars in the foreword he contributed to *Miftah Kunuz al-Sunnah*:

> "Had the Indian scholars not devoted themselves during these days to the study and development of the science of Hadith, this branch of learning would probably have disappeared altogether from the East since it had begun to be neglected and was on the decline in Egypt, Syria, Iraq and Arabia from the 10th century AH (15th century CE)."

The credit for the introduction, growth and popularisation of this field in India (particularly in northern and western India) rests with Shaykh Abdul Huq Muhaddith Dehlavi (d. 1642). By his learned translations and commentaries of the Hadith, by devoting over fifty years of his life to teaching them, and through other earnest endeavours, he established the science as a regular branch of study in India and earned for it the attention of the intellectual and literary circles. His pupils and descendants also took part in its propagation until, finally, Shah Waliullah and his family made it universally popular in the land.

In the modern era, the Indian ulema have produced highly meritorious commentaries on the Hadith which have won popular acclaim from near and far. Some of these are Maulana Muhammad Ashraf Dayanawi's *'Awn al-Ma'bud fi Sharh Sunan Abi Dawud*, Maulana Khalil Ahmad Saharanpuri's *Badhl al-Majhud fi Sharh Sunan Abi Dawud*,[27] Maulana Abdul Rahman Mubarakpuri's *Tuhfat al-Ahwadhi fi Sharh Sunan al-Tirmidhi*, Maulana Shabbir Ahmad Osmani's *Fath al-Mulhim fi Sharh Sahih Muslim*, and the great Hadith scholar Maulana Muhammad Zakariyya Kandhlawi's *Awjaz al-Masalik ila Sharh Muwatta' Imam Malik*. In addition to these, Maulana Anwar Shah Kashmiri's comments and annotations on *Sahih al-Bukhari*, published under the title of *Fayd al-Bari*, are looked upon as an invaluable treasure-house of knowledge on the subject of Hadith. Maulana Zaheer Ahsan Shauq Neemwi's unfinished work, *Aathar al-Sunan*, on the Hadith and the exposition of the Hanafi school of law also shows rare insight and understanding and makes a profound modern contribution to the study of Hadith. Sadly, premature death prevented the Maulana from completing the book, otherwise it would have surely been a memorable achievement in this field.[28]

Some Unique Contributions

Several books by Indian ulema have been regarded as unique in their subject throughout the world of Islam. Here we will mention just a few. Among the commentaries of the Quran, we have *Tafsir Mazhari* by Qadi Sanaullah Panipati (d. 1810). Then there are the three books of Maulana Rahmatullah Kairanwi (d. 1891), *Izhar al-Huq*, *Izalat al-Awham* and *Izalat al-Shukuk*, considered to be the best works in repudiating Christianity and critically assessing the Torah and the Bible. The ulema of Turkey, Egypt and Syria have prescribed Maulana Rahmatullah's books for student of the subject as well as for those who aspire to engage themselves in disputations with Christian missionaries. Repeated editions of them have been brought out in these countries. *Al-Fara'id* by Mullah Mahmud Jaunpuri (d. 1671) on eloquence, and Maulana Hamiduddin Farahi's (d. 1930) *al-Imam fi Aqsam al-Quran* and *Jawharat al-Balaghah*, along with his commentaries on the different chapters of the Quran, belong to the same category of writings. Justice Karamat Hussain's *Fiqh al-Lisan* and Maulana Syed Sulaiman Ashraf's *al-Mubin* also are admirable works on the philology of the Arabic language. Maulana Abdul Majid Daryabadi's commentary of the Quran (in English as well as Urdu) deserves a special mention among the modern contributions to the study of Islam. It is distinguished by the wealth of new information it contains on men and places mentioned in the Quran as obtained from recent archaeological findings and the author's deep research into Christianity and Judaism. It fulfils a great need in Islamic literature.

Apart from the Arabic language, Indian ulema have also produced literary and theological works in Persian and Urdu that are unsurpassed in value and importance. For instance, we have the great Shaykh Ahmad Sirhindi's *Maktubat* (letters) on higher religious and spiritual truths, Shah Waliullah's *Izalat al-Khafa'* on the principles of interpretation of the Quran, Shah Abdul Aziz's *al-Tuhfa al-Isna al-'Ashariyyah* in refutation of Shi'ism, Syed Ahmad Shaheed's *al-Sirat al-Mustaqim* on Islamic mysticism, Maulana Shah Ismail Shaheed Dehlavi's *Mansab Imamah* on the nature of imamate and the duties and qualifications of the imams and deputies of the Prophet (s), Maulana Muhammad Qasim Nanautawi's *Hujjat al-Islam* and *Taqrir-i-Dilpizir*, Maulana Abdul Shakoor Faruqi's books on the refutation of Shi'ism and his commentaries on certain chapters of the Quran, Maulana Syed Sulaiman Nadwi's *Sirat al-Nabi* and *Khutbat-i-Madras*, Qadi Muhammad Sulayman Mansurpuri's *Rahmatun lil-'Alamin* and Maulana Syed Manazir Ahsan Gilani's *al-Nabi al-Khatim* on the life of the Prophet and Maulana Shibli's *Sher al-'Ajam* on the history of Persian poetry. Many of these books have been translated into Turkish and Arabic.

Maulana Abdul Kalam Azad's writings were few and rather limited in their scope, nevertheless, he was a magician with the pen. He founded a new style of Urdu prose although it was not taken up after him. For his eloquence of expression and grandeur of style, which are the highlights of his *Tazkirah* and *Tarjuman al-Quran*, he will surely go down in the history of Urdu Literature as a great writer and a powerful stylist.

Among the works of Maulana Syed Abul A'la Mawdudi (who was born in India and who's literary career began and attained its fullness there) are a number of books, pamphlets and essays which are of outstanding value. The collections of his essays known as *Tanqihat* and *Tafhimat*, his books on purdah, jihad and usury are excellent examples of scholastic writing.

Islamic Literature in English

Indian Muslims were the first Muslims in the world to realise the need for producing Islamic literature in English. They had the closest contact with the English and saw clearly that, in order to teach Islam to non-Muslims and also western educated Muslims, it was necessary to publish standard books on Islam written in that language. Books written by Indians in English are regarded as the best and most useful vehicles for introducing Islam found in any western language and they are also the most widely read in the Muslim world. Some of the better known of these books are Syed Ameer Ali's *Spirit of Islam* and *History of the Saracens*, Khwaja Kanakuddin's *The Ideal Prophet* and *Sources of Christianity*, and Abdullah Yusuf Ali's *Commentary of the Quran*. Maulana Abdul Majid Daryabadi's recent *Commentary of the Quran* makes a most commendable addition to Islamic literature in English.

Hindi

In keeping with their historical tradition and the sense of pragmatism and generosity conferred on them by the liberal teachings of their faith, Muslims showed no prejudice towards the languages of Hindi and Bhasha. Although Arabic was their religious language and Persian their literary and court language, instead of treating Hindi as an alien tongue, they actually produced some excellent poetry and literature in it. Besides Amir Khusro and Abdul Rahim Khan-i-Khanan, Maulana Riqullah Dehlavi, the author of *Paimain* and *Joot Niranjan*, and Malik Muhammad Jaisi, who wrote the immortal *Padmavat*, command a position of unique importance in Hindi literature. There have also been a number of Hindi poets in Bilgram, as we learn from Maulana Ghulam Ali's *Sarv-i-Azad*. *Bang Darpan* was written by a Muslim poet of that very town and so was *Prem Prakash*. Shaykh Qasim of Daryabad (author of *Hans Jawahar*), Molvi Rahat Ali of Bijnor, Shah Qazim Qalandar of Kakori and Maulana Muhammad Zahir of Rae Bareli are among the numerous Muslims poets whose poems in Hindi are full of life and matters of the heart and represent literature of the highest value.

Arabic Language and Literature

From the very beginning, Indian Muslims showed a strong attachment to Arabic language and literature, cherishing it as a language of literary expression. There have been excellent Arabic poets among them, such as Qadi Abdul Muqtadir Kindi Dehlavi (d. 1388), Shaykh Ahmad ibn Muhammad Thanesari (d. 1417), Maulana Ghulam Ali Azad Bilgrami (d. 1785), Mufti Sadruddin Dehlavi (d. 1868), Maulana Faizul Hasan Saharanpuri (d. 1886), Maulana Zulfiqar Ali Deobandi (d. 1904), Muhammad Abbas Lakhnavi, Maulana Nasir Hasan Kintoori, Maulana Baqar Madrasi and Maulana Awhaduddin Bilgrami. Then there are Indian scholars like Professor Abdul Aziz Memon and Maulana Muhammad Surti, to whom Arabic scholars have paid unqualified homage for their command of the Arabic language. In acknowledgement of his ability as a linguist, the former was even appointed onto the committee setup to revise the most authoritative Arabic lexicon of all, *Lisan al-Arab*. His *Abu al-'Ala' wa ma ilayh* and his brilliant editing of *Simt al-La'ali* are indicative of his great erudition and mastery over the Arabic language.

Arabic Journalism
Even now, despite the loss of influence the Muslims in India have suffered, they are still clinging to the Arabic language. The standard books of Arabic learning and literature are included in the syllabi of their madrasahs, and a fair amount of literary work is being produced in it. From time to time, Arabic journals are published. Some time ago, *al-Bayan* used to be published from Lucknow under the joint editorship of Maulana Abdul Emadi and Molvi Abdul Razzaq Malihabadi. There was also Maulana Abul Kalam Azad's *al-Jam'iyyah* from Calcutta. In 1935, an Arabic magazine, called *al-Ridwan*, was started from Lucknow under the editorship of Hakim Muhammad Askari Naqvi, although it ceased publication after only four or five years. *Al-Diya'*, the Arabic magazine of Nadwatul Ulama, Lucknow, was read with interest in the literary quarters of the Arab world. It was edited by the late Maulana Masood Alam Nadwi whose proficiency in Arabic was acknowledged by the very best. Nowadays, a monthly Arabic magazine devoted to Islamic revival is being published by Nadwatul Ulama under the title of *al-Ba'th al-Islami*, and in addition, the students of that institution publish their own fortnightly Arabic journal, *al-Ra'id*. Recently, the Darul Uloom in Deoband also began publishing a monthly Arabic magazine called *al-Yaqazah*.

Present-day Writers in Arabic
Nadwatul Ulama has produced a number of Arabic writers and scholars who have earned a name even in the Arab countries for their literary endeavours. It is not possible for an impartial critic, looking at the various intellectual and literary movements of the modern Islamic world, to overlook the service of these scholars and writers. As writers, they have evolved a style of

their own, pleasantly combining literary charm, vitality of faith and traditional morality with the spontaneity and freshness of modern literature.

Chapter 3
Some Outstanding Muslim Personalities

Intrinsic Strength
The ability of a nation to produce individuals endowed with exceptional abilities in the different branches of human endeavour is a proof of its intrinsic strength and creative vitality. It shows that the sources of its thought and action have not yet run dry, that its spirit is still alive, and that it has not forfeited its right to exist with honour and dignity in the world. The Indian Muslims have reason to be proud of themselves in this respect. They have remained well-supplied with their share of outstanding individuals who have gloriously risen above the ordinary in their respective spheres of life.

The Exodus of Muslims following the Tartar Invasion
As soon as the foundations of a strong and enlightened Muslim Kingdom had been laid in India in the 12th century CE, scholars and skilled artists and craftsmen started to gather there from all parts of the Islamic world. Huge impetus was given to this immigration by the Tartar invasion of the Muslim East. The Tartars had

ravaged much of the Islamic Empire, but their wrath had fallen most ferociously on its capital, Baghdad, and on its other important centres of learning and culture. The result was that the pace of migration was greatly accelerated from the cities that had fallen victim to the barbarism of the Tartar and Mongol hordes. Educated and aristocratic families fled from one country to another in search of peace and security from the uncivilised invaders.

At that time, India was under the rule of monarchs belonging to what is known in history as the Slave Dynasty: a dynasty of Turkish slaves. It stood out as the only country that could hold the savage attackers at bay by successfully repelling their repeated inroads. Consequently, a large number of enlightened, high-class families from Iran and Afghanistan abandoned their homes and took refuge in India during this fearful time. Countless noblemen, who for generations had been distinguished by their learning and cultural refinement and who had held positions of honour and trust in their own countries, came to India to settle permanently. This happened particularly during the reigns of Shamsuddin Iltutmish, Ghiyasuddin Balban and Alauddin Khilji. Discussing this huge exodus and its causes, the renowned historian, Ziauddin Barni writes:

> "All these families of respected noblemen, accomplished scholars and exalted spiritual leaders left their homes and made their way towards India as a result of the invasions by the Mongols and by Chengiz Khan. Princes, experienced generals, celebrated teachers, learned jurists and illustrious religious and spiritual masters were all among the migrants."[29]

From these families, and from the families of Indians who had entered the fold of Islam through their efforts, came a steady stream of spiritual and intellectual luminaries, administrators, statesmen, army generals and conquerors. Among them, some were blessed with such exceptional greatness that they became a source of pride for the entire Muslim world.

Great Monarchs

One example of this is Sher Shah Suri, with his remarkable undertakings for public welfare, the vast developments he successfully completed, his splendid administrative achievements and revolutionary judicial reforms. When one considers that his rule barely extended over a five year period, one becomes convinced of the unique versatility and brilliance of this genius among kings. Some of his attainments during that brief span were so marvellous that many a well-established government would find it hard to accomplish them over a much longer period. Sher Shah is indeed one of greatest rulers the world has yet seen.

Marshman Clarke states:

> "He governed with the greatest beneficence, and the brief period of five years in which he held supreme power, is the most brilliant in the annals of India. He was a man of consummate ability, distinguished not less by his military exploits than by the triumphs of his civil administration. Though incessantly engaged in the field, he found time for a complete reform of every branch of the government, and his civil institutions survived his dynasty and became the model of those of Akbar."[30]

Then there is Akbar. Whatever the difference between the teachings of Islam and his own religious views and the *Din-i-Ilahi* he founded, and however much a Muslim historian may grieve at the intemperate developments that took place during the latter part of his reign, it goes without saying that he was a magnificent ruler and empire-builder when judged by his high-mindedness, legislative and administrative ability, conquests, natural knack for leadership and the splendid patronage he extended to the arts and learning.

Another ruler, for whom it is not easy to find an equal in history, is Aurangzeb. His excellent virtues of mind and character, his eventful life, with half a century of continuous warfare and incessant struggle, his vast conquests and far-reaching reforms, his simple, ascetic life, his matchless courage, fortitude and determination, the strict regularity of his hours, his management of a vast, sprawling empire, his personal command of armies on the battlefield, even in old age, his zealous observance of the obligatory as well as the supererogatory prayers, and his unceasing love for learning and study despite his incessant toil, mark him out as a man and emperor in a class of his own. He was a man who showed no fear, indecision or despair. As such, any impartial list of the greatest men of all time would include his name.

Another inspiring example of saintliness and scholarship can be seen in the life of Sultan Muzaffar Halim of Gujarat (d. 1525). His faith and sincerity, his piety and integrity, his asceticism, religious fervour and high-mindedness, and his prodigious scholarship is rarely seen, even in those who have nothing to do with kingship and statecraft and spend their lives exclusively in religious and literary pursuits. The following incident illustrates his excellent character and total selflessness. One historian of Gujarat states:

> "For a hundred years, the rulers of Malwa had tried in vain to make war on Gujarat. But when Mahmud Shah II of Malwa was deposed by his minister, Mandli Rai, and the rites of Islam there began to be wantonly outraged, the religious pride of Muzzaffar Shah, the King of Gujarat, was stirred. Setting out with a powerful army, he covered the distance to Malwa

with the utmost speed and besieged its fort. Realising that he was no match for the besieging force, Mandli Rai begged Rana Sanga to come to his aid. But before Rana Sanga could advance as far as Sarangpur, Muzaffar Shah dispatched a detachment of his valiant army to deal with him. Soon the fort of Malwa fell.

The sum and substance of the story is that, when Muzzaffar Shah entered the fort and the chiefs of his escort beheld the enormous wealth that the rulers of Malwa had amassed in it and heard accounts of the richness of the land, they ventured to suggest in his presence that since 2,000 of their horsemen had been killed in the fighting, it would not be wise to restore the kingdom back to the ruler who, owing to his incompetence, had lost it to his minister. As soon as Muzzaffar Shah had heard it, he cut short the round of inspection and came out of the fort, instructing Mahmud Shah not to allow any member of his party into the fort. The latter entreated him to stay on for a few days more, but he firmly declined. Explaining his action on a latter occasion, Mahmud Shah said, 'I had waged that war simply for the sake of earning the good pleasure of God. When I heard the conversation of the chiefs, I became apprehensive lest some unwholesome desire crop up in my heart to ruin the sincerity of my act. I have not done any favour to Mahmud Shah. On the contrary, I feel indebted to him for it was through him that I was given the opportunity of doing a noble deed.'[31]

As for his learning and his devotion to the Islamic sciences and the Hadith of the Prophet, it will suffice here to reproduce the following words from his 'acknowledgement of God's blessings', which he made a short while before his death. He states:

> "By the grace of God, in addition to knowing the Quran by heart, I have full understanding of the points of law arising out of every verse of it, the circumstances of its revelation and the method of its recitation. I remember by heart all the Hadith of the Prophet – their texts, references, the details of their narrators and everything. I possess such knowledge of *fiqh* (Islamic jurisprudence) that I hope to be a confirmation of the veracity of the Prophet's words that 'whoever God wishes to bless, He makes them a jurists of the religion'.
>
> I have now been engaged for some time in the purification of the self after the system of the Sufis and aspire for their blessings on the basis of the dictum: 'he who makes himself resembles a people (ultimately) becomes one of them.' I have finished reading *Tafsir Ma'alim al-Tanzil* once. I am now rereading it and have completed about half of it. I hope to complete the rest in Heaven."

As death approached, the following prayer of Prophet Yusuf[32] was on his lips:

> "My Lord! You have given me authority; You have taught me something about the interpretation of dreams; Creator of the heavens and the earth, You are my protector in this world and in the Hereafter. Let me die in true devotion to You. Join me with the righteous."
>
> (Quran: XII, 101)

Some Outstanding Muslim Personalities

Statesmen

Cutting short the story of kings and emperors, we will now take up the lives and attainments of some outstanding ministers and statesmen. The first individual of note is 'Imaduddin Gilani (d. 1481), known as Mahmud Gawan. Besides being an administrator and statesmen of exceptional brilliance, he was also a man of profound learning and a noted writer. Thus he combined both temporal and spiritual greatness, being without equal in devoutness, piety and administrative acumen. His fame spread as far as Iran, Arabia and Turkistan.

The life of Abul Qasim Abdul Aziz Gujarati (d. 1515), who is famous by the name of Asaf Khan and served as Minister of Gujarat, offers another astounding example of excellence and versatility. Shahabuddin Ibn Hajar al-Makki, the most important Arab scholar of that time, wrote a book on him, in which he paid glowing tributes to his immense learning and spiritual merit. In it he states:

> "A peculiar glow came over Mecca during the period of Asaf Khan's stay. The wise and the learned considered it a privilege to converse with him. There was a great fostering of learning..."

Several panegyrics were written in his praise by Arabian poets, and a mournful elegy was written by a distinguished Arab poet on his death.[33]

The renowned Mughal commander-in-chief, Abdul Rahim Khan-i-Khana wrote exquisite poems in Persian, Arabic and Hindi. Apart from being a literary critic of a high order, he was equally proficient with the pen and the sword, being an excellent linguist. One respected historian says of him:

> "His intelligence and sagacity, his magnanimity and

high mindedness, his liberality and munificence were beyond words. He was excessively fond of poetry and literature and was a voracious reader, particularly of historical books. He admired greatly the company of men of learning and excellence and shunned those who were otherwise. His life was one of piety and rigid self-discipline. He loved being magnanimous and shunned triviality. He was extremely versatile, possessing such a diversity of virtues that the like of him cannot be found."[34]

In the same way, Abdul Razzaq Khawafi has observed in *Ma'athir al-Umara'* that:

"Abdul Rahim Khan stands unrivalled among his contemporaries for courage and generosity. He enjoyed mastery over Persian, Arabic and Hindi. He could converse freely and compose beautiful verses in all the three languages."

Abdul Rahim Khan was a celebrated Hindi poet, and remains so to this day. He was also a leading poet in Persian, but the breadth and variety of his talent affected the quality of his Persian poetry. Had he dedicated himself exclusively to it, he would, no doubt, have reached the status of any of the Iranian poets at his court, whose poetry is still held in high regard.

Two other illustrious members of Akbar's court were Abul Fazl and Fyzee. Irrespective of their religious and spiritual views and the harm they did thereby to the cause of Islam in India, they were without doubt among the most outstanding men of their time, not only in India but in the whole literary world. Both of them were gifted with exceptional mental faculties, a rare love of learning and an extraordinary poetic and literary taste and aptitude. Fyzee deserves a place among the all-time masters of Iran for his Persian poetry, while Abul Fazl's *Ain-i-Akbar* and *Akbarnama* are marvels of knowledge and wisdom, observation and analysis. Carra de Vaux states regarding *Akbarnama*:

> "*Akbarnama* is an extraordinary literary work; it is overflowing with life, ideas and facts. A study of it reveals that all the fields of human existence have been thoroughly examined and the conclusions thus reached have been critically arranged and analysed. The eyes are dazzled by the continuous evolution of ideas it contains. It is a literary document of which the entire oriental civilisation can be proud. The persons whose mighty intellects have introduced themselves through this voluminous book seem to be far ahead of their age in administration and state craft, and not only in administration and statecraft, but religious philosophy as well. These poets and thinkers saw the material world with a highly penetrating eye. They were given to observe everything very deeply and to preserve in their minds what they saw. They used to experience everything personally and examine their own views and notions against the background of facts. On the one hand, their mode of expression was rich and eloquent, and, on the other, they supported and fortified their statements with facts and figures."[35]

One Solitary Exception

A sort of intellectual stagnation had come over the Muslim world after the Mongol invasion. Minds had become sterile and blindly imitative, and intellectual activity was brought almost to a standstill. The picture of degeneration becomes complete with the approach of the 14th century when lethargy and inertia also crept into the other branches of life. With a few exceptions, like Ibn Khaldun, the Islamic world could not produce anyone during this period who was above this general level of mediocrity. India, however, due to its physical remoteness, to some extent managed to escape the ravages of this decay. The Tartars, who had descended upon the world of Islam, bringing ruin and destruction in their wake, could not spread their grip all over India because of its geographical isolation. Consequently, a large number of the Muslim world's finest minds sought safety by migrating to India and settling down as permanent citizens. As a result, intellectual activity in India progressed for a considerable length of time. Lively endeavours continued to be in evidence in the literary field, and men of learning and wisdom continued to emerge who can rightfully be ranked among the foremost thinkers and scholars of Islam. For example, in the writings of Sharafuddin Yahya Maneri (d. 1370), Shah Waliullah Dehlavi (d. 1762), Shah Rafiuddin Dehlavi (d. 1817) and Shah Ismail Shaheed Dehlavi (d. 1817), one finds a level of originality that is generally absent from the works of their contemporaries in other parts of the Muslim world.

Reform and Renovation
Owing to various natural and historical factors, which we propose to discuss in the third volume of our *Saviours of Islamic Spirit*,[36] India became the nerve-centre of religious and spiritual reform during the declining phase of Islamic rule. Proselytising and reform activities made such an advance in India that many other countries became influenced by them. Here were born the foremost Islamic preachers and reformers. This was due to their earnestness and learning, their popularity and the great number of people who profited by their efforts, and their natural harmony with the true spirit of Islam.

The most elevated among these religious guides and redeemers was Shaykh Ahmad Sirhindi (d. 1624), upon whom men of

Some Outstanding Muslim Personalities

vision and understanding have conferred the title of *Mujaddid al-Alf al-Thani* (the Reviver of the Second Millennium). He renewed and strengthened the bond of Indian Muslims with Islam and saved the Sharia from being corrupted by innovations and the apostasy of extremist Sufis, who were openly inclined towards the pantheistic doctrine of *wahdat al-wujud* (God is everything and everything is God). He rescued the Mughal Empire from its spreading irreligiosity and put a check on the highly dangerous movement seeking the amalgamation of all faiths, as well as on the revival of Brahmanism.

The great worshipper and warrior for God's cause, Aurangzeb, was also a product of his mighty struggle. The Sufi order founded by him still endures, not just in India, but in Turkey, Iraq, Iran, Kurdistan, Syria and other parts of the world. The popularity this Sufi order later acquired, in Arabia, Kurdistan, Syria and Turkey, through the efforts of Shaykh Khalid Shahrazori Kurdi (d. 1826) has not been achieved by any other Sufi order.[37]

Then there was Syed Ahmad Shaheed who so splendidly reawakened the spirit of jihad among the Muslims of India. He stirred them to make heroic sacrifices for the sake of Islam and the establishment of a truly Islamic government after the manner of the Rightly Guided Caliphs.[38] As a result of his struggle, a wave of uprightness and devotion swept over the Muslims, and a new life of faith and endeavour, like that of the early days of Islam, was breathed into the dead body of the Indian part of the Ummah. He endowed his followers with rare piety and enthusiasm, while their religious steadfastness, scrupulous observance of the Sharia and ardent zeal for jihad were simply unique.[39] Nawab Siddiq Hasan Khan writes about Syed Ahmad Shaheed and the splendid men he collected around himself:

> "... the gist of the matter is that a man of his stature has not been heard of in the current age in any part of

the world, nor has a fraction of what his haloed band has done for the Muslims been achieved by any of the contemporary religious teachers or divines."[40]

In the modern era, India has once again become the centre of Islamic propagation and reform. It began under the inspired leadership of Maulana Muhammad Ilyas of Delhi (d. 1943). Throughout out travels in Muslim countries we have not come across a more staunch and fervent preacher of Islam than him. His special distinction lay in his absolute reliance upon God and total dedication to the cause of Islamic revival and resurgence.[41]

The missionary movement founded by Maulana Muhammad Ilyas is now actively at work in all parts of the Muslim world and parties of preachers are sent out regularly, even to far-off lands like the United States, European countries and Japan. This movement has succeeded to some degree in rekindling the flame of faith in the hearts of Muslims.

These are but a handful of instances of men of endeavour, faith and learning that arose from among the Indian Muslims to leave an indelible mark on the world. The eight volumes of *Nuzhat al-Khawatir* contain an account of some 5,000 Muslims of confirmed excellence in various walks of life who sprang from the Indian soil. It shows the limitless capacity of this land of ours to generate individuals of exceptional ability and calibre in all branches of human activity.

The sapling of Islam which the early Muslims planted on the Indian soil with their hands and nourished with their life-blood is still in bloom. Throughout their existence, the Indian Muslims have produced personalities that have been the envy of the world. Even under British rule, where there was a deliberate policy to devastate them intellectually and economically,[42] they continued to produce eminent legists, administrators, mathematicians, educationists and brilliant masters of the English language whose proficiency and skill was acknowledged even by Englishmen. The Indian Muslims have produced world-class leaders, legislators, debaters and orators. Their thinkers and poets have become famous in Afghanistan, Iran and Turkey, and their works have been translated into multiple foreign languages.

At the same time, they have always revered Arab culture and civilisation and made their own contribution to it. Given the prevailing trends, a new mode of thought and expression seems set to evolve in Arabic literature under the influence of Indian writers, one richly representative of both literary and spiritual values.

The glorious past of the Muslims of India suggests a bright future. As they currently pass through the most critical phase of their history, Indian Muslims are determined to ensure for themselves an honourable place in the Indian nation. Their spirit endures.

Chapter 4

Sufi Saints of India and Their Impact on Society

Sufi Orders

Although the chief Sufi orders had their origins outside India, they attained their greatest success here. This is partly due to historical circumstances and partly as a result of the Indian character and temperament. From these orders, fraternities developed in India which themselves grew into permanent orders and recognised schools of Islamic mysticism. Apart from the well-known Qadiriyyah, Chishtiyyah, Naqshbandiyyah, and Suhrawardiyyah orders, there are other orders and fraternities that are essentially Indian and are attributed solely to men who were born and died in India. For instance, the Madariyyah, Qalandariyyah, the Shattariyah and the Mujaddidiyah orders. India has been the standard-bearer of *Tasawwuf* (Islamic mysticism) and spiritual evolution and self-reform since the 17th century.

It was at that time that a countless number of people profited spiritually from Shaykh Ahmad Sirhindi and his illustrious son and successor, Khwaja Muhammad Masoom. Deputies of the latter were found in several foreign countries, including Iran, Afghanistan and Turkistan.

Likewise, votaries from Turkey, Baghdad, Syria, Samarqand, Bukhara, Egypt, China and Ethiopia were drawn to the *khanqah*[43] of the 19th century saint of the Mujaddidiyah order, Shah Ghulam Ali Dehlavi. The Mujaddidiyah order was popularised in Iraq, Syria, Kurdistan and Turkey by Shaykh Ghulam Ali's deputy, Maulana Khalid Rumi, and it still endures in these places.

Then, at the beginning of the 20th century, it was the turn of Hajji Imdadullah Muhajir to reach such heights, becoming known popularly in the Islamic world as the 'Spiritual Guide of the Arabs and the non-Arabs'. Countless Arabs and pilgrims availed themselves of his priceless spiritual guidance during his stay in that country.

Even in the contemporary Muslim world, it is India which is keeping the spirit of Islam alive. An uninterrupted chain of earnest and exalted men of God has enabled India to maintain its distinction as the universal centre of spiritual and Sufi endeavour. It is now the primary refuge in the world for the votaries of Sufism.

Popular Enthusiasm
The Muslim era in India's history was, in fact, heralded by the Sufi saints, particularly Khwaja Moinuddin Ajmeri, who laid the foundations of the Chishtiyyah order there. From the earliest days, the rich vied with the poor and the high with the low to pay homage to these elevated self-denying men of God. As a result, the whole subcontinent became lit by a throng of spiritual luminaries and their religious establishments. Over and above the more important towns, there was hardly a Muslim hamlet which was left without a moral teacher or spiritual guide.

People's enthusiastic devotion to the Sufi saints can be ascertained from the following information.

The average number of votaries staying at the *khanqah* of Syed Adam Bannuri (d. 1643) was one thousand. They took their meals at the *khanqah*. A great throng of men, including hundreds of scholars, followed the saint wherever he went. It is stated in *Tazkira-i-Adamiya* that 10,000 people formed his entourage during his visit to Lahore in 1642. Seeing the phenomenal popularity of Syed Bannuri, Emperor Shah Jahan became so apprehensive that he thought of a plan to send him out of India. He sent him a large sum of money and then suggested that, as having wealth makes the pilgrimage obligatory, he should waste no time in performing the obligation. Thereupon, the saint migrated from India.

His celebrated son and spiritual deputy, Khwaja Muhammad Masoom (d. 1668), had as many as 9,000 disciples who gave him *bay'ah*[44] and offered repentance at his hands. Of these, 7,000 rose to be his *khalifahs*.[45]

Regarding Shah Ghulam Ali, Sir Syed Ahmad Khan records in his *Asar-us-Sanadeed* that: "not less than 500 destitute individuals used to live in his *khanqah*, all of whom were fed and clothed by him."

Unprecedented scenes of popularity were witnessed during the missionary tours of the famous saint and spiritual leader of the 19th century Syed Ahmad Shaheed. The same was to also occur during his journey to Calcutta while on his way to Arabia for the Hajj. In many of the towns on the route, there remained only a few people who did not give him *bay'ah* and offer repentance at his hand. At Allahabad, Mirzapur, Varanasi, Ghazipur, Azimabad (Patna) and Calcutta especially, his disciples must have run into hundreds of thousands. At Varanasi, the patients at the Sadar hospital sent a petition begging him to visit them in the hospital so that they could offer the *bay'ah*, as they were unable to come out. About a thousand people became his disciples every day during his two months' stay at Calcutta.

From morning until late at night, a stream of men and women would pour in to the place he was staying, such that there was hardly any time left for him to attend to his personal needs. When it became impossible to accept the vow from everyone individually, it was arranged for people to gather in a large house where Syed Ahmad Shaheed went and initiated them into the fold. Seven or eight turbans were unrolled on the ground, and the aspirants were told to hold them at different places, while one end of them was held by Syed Ahmad Shaheed himself. He then taught them the fundamentals of the faith and read out the oath in a loud voice as if calling the *Adhan*[46] which they repeated, and thus the ritual was completed. This was done seventeen or eighteen times each day.

Social Significance

The virtuous Sufis would call upon those taking *bay'ah* at their hands to offer earnest repentance for their sins and make a solemn affirmation of loyalty and obedience to God and the Prophet. They would warn them against licentiousness and self-indulgence, injustice, oppression and violation of the rights of others. These pious teachers focused on the moral elevation of their disciples by prescribing measures for eradicating vices like vanity, malice, jealousy and lust for wealth and power. They urged them to remember God, to treat His creatures well, and to practice self-denial and contentment. Besides the *bay'ah*, which symbolised the forging of a special link between the guide and the disciple, the revered teachers also encouraged and counselled whoever came to them. They sought to awaken in their hearts a love for the Divine and an ambition to seek His pleasure and to strive with all their might for their own self-correction and inner reform.

Through their tremendous sincerity, moral excellence, preaching and instruction, Sufi leaders exercised a powerful, inspiring and morally regenerating influence on society. This is illustrated in the following extract by the renowned historian, Ziauddin Barni, where he depicts the social conditions prevailing in India during the reign of Alauddin Khilji:

> "The leading Sufi saints at the time of Alauddin Khilji were Shaykh-ul-Islam Nizamuddin, Shaykh-ul-Islam Alauddin and Shaykh-ul-Islam Ruknuddin. The world received enlightenment from them and took the *bay'ah* at their hands. Sinners were inspired by them to repent from their sins and thousands of evildoers and people who habitually missed their prayers abandoned their evil ways and became devout worshippers; a strong fervour was created among them for religious deeds and their repentance attained perfection. The obligatory duties of worship and the divine ordinances in the other spheres of life began to be observed as a matter of course. Excessive attachment to worldly desires and aspirations, which lies at the root of most evils, was reduced under the force of the high morality, asceticism and profound self-denial of these spiritual masters... people grew truthful as a result of their blessings; they became honest in the management of worldly affairs and were fired by ambition to improve and evolve their inner selves due to the inspirational influence exercised by the laudable moral conduct, abstinence and spirituality of the Sufi leaders..."

The historian goes on to say:

> "In the last years of Sultan Alauddin's rule, the general moral level had improved so much that a majority of the people abstained from drink, adultery, gambling and other social and moral perversions. The major sins were shunned as equivalent to infidelity. Muslims refrained from open usury and hoarding for fear of each other's censure. Adulteration, deceit and under-weighing were eliminated from the market."[47]

It is not possible in these few pages to give a coherent, historical picture of the reformation brought about by the Sufi saints. They made an enormous contribution towards the evolution of a healthy, conscientious environment in India. This has been the nation's greatest asset, and it has provided it with worthy leaders and redeemers at every critical point of history. Leaving aside the intervening centuries, details of which are contained in the memoirs and biographies of the spiritual leaders, we will examine an incident from the life of Syed Ahmad Shaheed, a religious reformer and Sufi saint of the 19th century. This will demonstrate the extent of the moral impact that his personality had on society. It is recorded in connection with his brief stay in Calcutta that:

> "The liquor business in that great city was suddenly brought to a standstill. The liquor merchants complained to the authorities that though they were paying taxes regularly, they had been forced to close down their businesses since the arrival in the city of a saint under whose influence more and more Muslims were being reformed daily and taking the vow not to indulge in intoxicants any more. They did not even look at the liquor shops now."[48]

The venerable saints enjoined the new entrants into their orders to be fair in monetary dealings, pay back any debts and to be scrupulous in satisfying the claims of others. To cite one example, Khwaja Nizamuddin Awliya was emphatically told by his spiritual mentor, Khwaja Fariduddin Ganj Shakar, "to always do his level best to placate his opponent and render to everyone his due." Khwaja Nizamuddin Awliya owed one person some money and had lost a book he had borrowed from another. On arriving in Delhi, he went to settle these accounts, the person to whom he owed the money remarked, "It seems you are coming from the society of the Muslims," while the owner of the book said, "It is always like this at the place from where you are coming."[49]

Likewise, under the guidance and instruction of the Sufi saints, people were imbued with the desire to please and help others. During the long Hajj journey, Syed Ahmad Shaheed and his large band of companions missed no opportunity to do any act of public service. While sailing down the Ganges, they came across a boat at Mirzapur which was laden with cotton. The owner of the cotton needed laborers to unload it. Seeing his plight, Syed Ahmad, told his companions to unload the boat and they did it so energetically that the task was completed in a couple of hours. Those seeing this were amazed, commenting: "What sort of men are these? They didn't even know the cotton merchant and yet they worked so hard for him without charging a penny. These are truly devout men of God."[50]

The moral growth achieved by the Sufi saints in India was solely the result of their level of spirituality and good character. No government, law, or other institution could bring about such an improvement in so many people or keep them so steadily within the bounds of moral propriety and rectitude.

Fearlessness

One valuable service that the Sufi saints performed was to fearlessly stand up against the unjust and immoral ways of any tyrannical rulers. They saved their kingdom and society in general from the consequences of the follies of these rulers by boldly telling the truth to their faces. Inspired by their example, others lost their fear and became courageous. The history of Muslim rule in India offers any number of instances when Muslim saints put aside their own personal safety and, risking their lives, fulfilled the Islamic duty contained in the Prophet's hadith that the greatest form of jihad is to speak the truth to a tyrannical ruler.

Shaykh Qutbuddin Munawwar was a Chishti saint who lived

in solitude during the reign of Muhammad ibn Tughluq. Once the king, on one of his tours, chanced to pass through the area where the saint lived, but the saint did not come to meet him. The king then summoned him to Delhi. When the Shaykh entered the royal palace, the court nobles, ministers, heralds and attendants were standing in a double row in front of the throne. On seeing the imposing spectacle, his young son, Nuruddin, who was with him, and had never been in a king's court before, was seized with fright. The Shaykh admonished him sternly; "Glory is for God, Baba Nuruddin," he said to him in a loud voice. The son related later that as soon as he had heard these words, he felt a new strength surging within him; all his fear disappeared, and the court grandees began to look to him as meek as goats. The king complained to the saint: "When I was in your neighbourhood, you neither counselled me nor honoured me with a visit." The Shaykh replied, "The dervish[51] does not consider himself worthy of royal society. In his solitary corner he prays for the king as for the general body of Muslims. He will now beg to be excused." After the interview, the King confided to a nobleman that he had noticed with all spiritual leaders with whom he had occasion to shake hands, that their hands trembled at the time, but Shaykh Munawwar's grip was so firm that he seemed to be completely unaffected by the event. The king then gifted him a purse of 100,000 gold coins, whereupon the Shaykh exclaimed: "Glory be to God! Two measures[52] of pulses and rice and a piece of ghee are enough for the dervish. What will he do with all this money?" After considerable persuasion and on being advised that the king would be irritated by a blank refusal, he agreed to accept 2,000 pieces. These he distributed among his brother-saints and other poor and indigent people, before returning from Delhi.[53]

    Another saint who had a strong aversion to meeting Sultan Muhammad ibn Tughluq was Maulana Fakhruddin Zarradi. He often used to say that he saw his head rolling in the Sultan's court, i.e. he would not hesitate to speak the truth and the king would not forgive him. At last, he was called by the Sultan to his court. "Give me some good advice," the sultan said. "Suppress anger," the Maulana said. "What anger?" the Sultan asked. "The anger of wild beasts," the Maulana replied. The King grew red in the face at the reply, but he kept quiet. After this, the royal meal was ordered. The king shared his vessel with the Maulana and even fed him with his own hand. The Maulana ate with apparent dislike. When the meal was over, the Maulana came away.[54]

The Sufi saints steadfastly upheld the traditions of detachment, fearlessness and championing the truth, even though those were the days of absolute monarchy and despotic rule. The king, too, under the force of their spirituality, felt compelled to allow them the freedom to perform their duty, even when they showed no consideration for these forthright and honest ulema. The spiritual leaders zealously guarded their self-respect and dignity before mighty rulers, chieftains and noblemen right up to the last days of the Mughal Empire. It is reported that Emperor Shah Alam was once present in the Mehfil-e-Sama[55] of Khwaja Mir Dard when, troubled by a painful leg, he could not help stretching it a little. The Khwaja protested: "It is against the decorum of the society of the *faqir*[56] to sit like this." The emperor apologised and indicated his discomfort, upon which Khwaja Mir Dard remarked, "If you were not feeling well, what was the need to come?"[57]

Propagation of Knowledge and Learning

The Sufis of India were great patrons of learning, some of them being outstanding men of letters themselves. Their belief was that it was impossible to know God without knowledge, and also that 'an ignorant Sufi is the Devil's plaything.' There are instances when they refused to admit into their folds votaries of striking promise and aptitude until they had completed their education. As we will see in detail in a later chapter, the remarkable educational and literary progress of India under the Muslims was due, directly or indirectly, to the encouragement given by the Sufi saints. Two of the greatest scholars and teachers of the 14th century, Qadi Abdul Muqtadir Kindi and Shaykh Ahmad Thanesari, were the spiritual protégés of Khwaja Nasiruddin Chiragh Dehlawi. The renowned 17th century educationist and teacher Maulana Lutfullah of Kora Jahanabad was a Sufi saint of the Chishtiyyah order. Through his pupils, and subsequent generations of their pupils, educational activity was kept going until the 19th century. Often, the *khanqah* and madrasah complemented each other. The Khanqah i Rashidiyyah of Jaunpur, the madrasah of Shah Waliullah at Delhi and the *khanqah* of Maulana Rashid Ahmad at Gangoh were the best examples of this.

Benevolence

The needs of thousands of men used to be satisfied through the saints, and in countless homes hearts came to life through their benevolence. A vast number of people lived in their *khanqahs* as permanent guests enjoying all the reasonable comforts of life. At the dinner tables of the Sufi ascetics, no distinction was made between rich or poor, friend or foe, kindred or stranger. The dinner table of Khwaja Nizamuddin Awliya was proverbial both for its extensiveness and the sumptuousness of the meals served on it. At the *khanqah* of Shaykh Saifuddin Sirhindi, a Mujaddidiyyah saint of the 17th century, 1,400 people used to dine every day and every one of them was served with food of his own choice.[58]

It is reported in the biography of another Chishti saint of the late 17th and early 18th centuries, Syed Muhammad Saeed, known as Shah Bheek, that apart from the 5,000 votaries who lived permanently in his *khanqah*, an equal number of daily visitors also joined in the meals, meaning that about 1,000 people dined with him regularly. Once, Roshan-ud-Daula, who was a Seh-Hazari[59] feudal lord of the Court of Emperor Farrukh Siyar of Delhi, presented him with 70,000 rupees for the construction of the *khanqah*. The Shah advised him to leave the money and go and have a little rest as the work would commence in the afternoon. After Roshan-ud-Daula had retired Shah Bheek sent the entire money to widows and other needy and indigent people of Ambala, Thanesar, Sirhind and Panipat, through the ascetics of the *khanqah*. When Roshan-ud-Daula returned in the afternoon, Shah Saheb said to him: "You could never have earned so much Divine reward by the construction of a *khanqah* as you have by serving so many poor, helpless persons and hermits. What would a humble ascetic like me do with a palatial building?" On another occasion, Emperor Farrukh Siyar, Roshan-ud-Daula and Nawab Abdullah Khan sent him promissory notes worth 300,000 rupees along with their petition. The saint had all the money distributed in the neighbouring towns and among indigent families of good birth.[60] As Maulana Manazir Ahsan Gilani has very appropriately observed:

> "The *khanqahs* of Sufi saints served as the connecting link between the rich and the poor. Even reigning monarchs paid tribute to the courts of these august men. Take the case of Sultan al-Mashayikh; it has been shown how Khizr Khan, the heir-apparent to the throne of Delhi, was his devoted disciple. Sultan Alauddin Khilji used to collect the tribute from all parts of the country, but there was one treasury in which he also had to deposit the money submitted... The *khanqahs* were the channels through which the share of the poor and the needy used to reach them throughout the land. This is what was implied by the well-known saying: 'the property of the Sufi is at everyone's disposal.'

This confluence of poverty and riches, i.e., the holy orders of the Sufis, to which the rich and the poor alike paid homage, was the agency through which the needs of innumerable destitute Muslim families were satisfied. Indeed, there was no phase in the whole era of Muslim supremacy in India, and no province in the entire subcontinent, in which the Prophet's command: 'it should be taken from those among them that are rich and given to those among them that are poor' was not dutifully carried into practice by the Sufi saints, especially by those among them who, by some extraordinary circumstance, had come to acquire influence over the rich and privileged sections of the community; the fortune of the distressed sections would, then, literally wake up."[61]

Resignation and Contentment

The saintly Sufis generally abstained from accepting offices of the State or gifts or grants from wealthy lords, princes and other well-to-do people. By their conduct, they established a tradition of sublime asceticism, contentment, reliance upon God and self-respect, which encouraged and sustained the ideals of magnanimity, open-mindedness and integrity in the general Indian society. Human honour and dignity became valued, in a world where even human beings are bought and sold. Their guiding principle and open declaration in this regard was:

> I shall not exchange my tattered pallet for a royal standard,
> Nor my poverty[62] for Solomon's domains;
>
> The treasure I have discovered in my heart because of poverty's pang,

I shall not exchange for the comforts of kings.

There is practically no Sufi order which does not abound in glorious stories of the triumph of spiritual values over worldly and materialistic urges and temptations. Here, however, we will quote instances only from the last two centuries to show on what a lofty plane the Sufis continued to operate, even when materialism had become rife in Indian society and spiritual values were at a disadvantage everywhere.

Mirza Mazhar Jan-i-Janan was a Sufi leader of the Naqshbandiya Mujaddidiya order. The emperor of Delhi approached him with a request to accept something from the vast Empire that God had blessed him with. He replied: "God has said about the kingdom of the seven climes (i.e. the habitable world) that the stock of the world is meagre. Of it only a country of one clime has come into your possession. How much can it be that I extended a covetous hand towards it?" Once Nawab Asaf Jah presented him with 20,000 rupees, which he refused. The Nawab urged him to accept, saying: "Take them and give them away to the poor." Mirza Jan-i-Janan replied, "Start distributing them as you proceed from here and they will be used up by the time you are back home. If any of them are left, they will be finished there."

Nawab Mir Khan, the ruler of Tonk (in Rajasthan), wanted to make a grant for the maintenance of the *khanqah* of Shah Ghulam Ali of Dehli. When he came to know of the ruler's intentions, the Sufi had this verse written to him:

> We do not disgrace resignation and contentment,
> Tell Mir Khan, one's portion is pre-ordained.

Once a high-ranking government officer who had come to meet Maulana Shah Fazlur Rahman of Ganj Moradabad (d. 1895) was so impressed by the high moral level of his conversation that he said, "If you are willing, I can move the Government to bestow a grant on your *khanqah*." The Maulana observed, "What will I do with the grant of your Government? By the grace of God, I have a stringed cot, two earthen *lotas*[63] and two pitchers of clay. Some disciples bring me a little millet from which bread is made, and my wife cooks some pulses or cheap vegetables with which I eat the bread."

Again it is related by Molvi Muhibullah that Nawab Kalb-i-Ali Khan of Rampur once expressed the desire that the Maulana honour him with a visit. Molvi Muhibullah asked what would he offer to the Maulana if he came, to which he replied, "100,000 rupees." Molvi Muhibullah then went to Ganj Moradabad to persuade the Maulana to undertake the journey. "Come to Rampur," he pleaded with him, "Nawab Kalb-i-Ali is very eager to have you as his guest. He will make a present of 100,000 rupees if you go there." The Maulana heard as if it mattered absolutely nothing to him and then he said, "Forget the 100,000 (rupees), and listen to this:

> When I behold His favours on my heart to
> me it appears
> far more precious than the cup of Jamshed."

A Refuge for Humanity

People became imbued with high humanitarian ideals in the company of the Sufis. They gained a deep concern for humanity and sought to offer whatever service they could to their fellow men without regard for their race or creed. They believed in, and fashioned their conduct on the Prophet's advice that "God's creatures are his family; among His slaves, He loves most whoever serves his family with the greatest devotion."

Khwaja Nizamuddin Awliya is reported to have said about himself that "when a person comes to me and relates his troubles I feel twice as much distressed as him."[64] Another of his favourite dictums was: "On the Day of judgment, nothing will carry greater weight than the desire to serve and to please."[65]

Many a weary and broken-hearted soul would find refuge in the *khanqahs* of the saints. The arms of the revered Sufis were always open to welcome those that had been jilted by fate or who had been forsaken by their kinsmen and society. The dejected, the anguished and the outcast would come to them and find shelter, food, love and recognition. They would find balm for their broken hearts and wounded spirits. When the spiritual guide and mentor of Khwaja Nizamuddin Awliya was sending him off finally to settle in Delhi, he bestowed this blessing upon him: "You will be like a huge, shady tree under which God's creatures will find comfort."[66] History bears witness to the fact that for a full seventy years people came from far and near and found shelter and protection under his benevolent shadow. Thanks to the Sufi ascetics, there existed in hundreds of places in India such 'huge, shady, trees' under whose merciful shade broken travellers used to find new life and freedom.

Chapter 5
Indo-Islamic Culture

Two Determining Factors
The cultural structure of Muslims everywhere is determined by two major factors: (i) the Islamic belief, way of life and code of ethics; and (ii) the indigenous civilisation and local customs, which are bound to make their influence felt. The first constituent – the Islamic belief, way of life and code of ethics – is the common attribute of the cultural makeup of Muslims all over the world. Wherever they may be living, and whatever their language or dress, this attribute is shared by them universally. By virtue of it, they form a single brotherhood in spite of the many things that differentiate them locally. The other component signifies that part of their culture which distinguishes them from their co-religionists living in other parts of the world and imparts to them their individual national character.

Indian Muslims are not exempt from this general principle. Their culture, which has taken centuries to evolve, is a combination of both Islamic and Indian influences. This duality has endowed it with a beauty and richness which is characteristically all its own. At the same time, it has ensured that this culture can operate here, not as an alien or a traveller, but as a natural, permanent citizen, who has built his home taking into account his particular needs and circumstances, past traditions and new impulses, while making an enduring contribution to the native environment surrounding him. To seek to deprive a person of the transcendental values and ethical ideals common between him and large portions of humanity is like attempting to supress his spirituality and destroy his universal outlook. In the same way, it is utterly futile and unjust to expect him to cut himself loose from his environment and lead a life completely detached from local influences.

Characteristics of the Abrahamic Civilisation

From the point of view of Islamic belief, morality and way of life, Indian Muslims, along with Muslims of all other lands, possess a distinctive civilisation for which there can be no more appropriate and comprehensive title than Abrahamic[67] Civilisation. This civilisation has three essential attributes which have fixed their stamp on its entire spiritual, intellectual and social design and have given it a flavour and character that are manifestly its own. These three attributes are: God-consciousness, monotheism (taught ceaselessly by all the Prophets belonging to the lineage of Prophet Ibrahim, a complete elaboration of which is contained in the Quran), and a permanent, natural awareness of human dignity and equality that never deserts the mind of a Muslim. It is these characteristics which lend a distinctive personality to the Abrahamic Civilisation. As far as we can say, in no other system of civilisation are these features so strikingly in evidence.

The Place of God in the Life of a Muslim

Faith in the existence of God, a constant awareness of Him, and a ready expression of this awareness are fundamental and inalienable constituents of the life and culture of Muslims. Islamic Civilisation can aptly be compared to a dress which is worn in different styles at different places according to the taste, climate and other conditions prevailing there; however, its texture is the same everywhere and it is dyed in the same hue so deep that every tissue and fibre is totally impregnated with it. The name of God and His remembrance run like blood in the veins and arteries of Islamic Civilisation. When a child is born in a Muslim home, the first ceremony it undergoes, within a few minutes of its birth, is the *adhan*[68] being recited into its ears. Thus, the first name it becomes familiar with, even before it acquires its own name, is that of God. On the seventh day, the *aqiqa*[69] is performed, at which a name is given to the child; the choice generally falling on one which expresses the sentiment of loyalty to God or proclaims His absolute unity and oneness, or is patterned after the names of that most exalted group of monotheists, the Prophets, or their pupils or immediate disciples. When the time comes for the child to begin his education and go to school, it is celebrated with the recitation of the name of God and a few verses from the Holy Quran.[70] This ceremony is known among Indian Muslims as Tasmiya Khwani or Bismillah.

At the time of marriage, again, the name of God is invoked to unite together in a permanent bond two mature and responsible people, who pledge to uphold the prestige of that name throughout their lives.

The wedding sermon is delivered in the manner sanctified by the Prophet's practice, expressing gratitude to God for having created the human race in pairs of men and women and exhorting the couple to live and die in a state of faithfulness to Him.

When the auspicious day of Eid al-Fitr[71] arrives, a Muslim is called upon to raise his voice in the affirmation of His glory and greatness (Allahu Akbar) and offer two *rakahs*[72] of prayers in thanksgiving, after bathing himself and putting on clean clothes.

On Eid-ul-Adha,[73] he is required to offer up an animal sacrifice in God's name.

Finally, when the ultimate stage of life's journey is reached, a Muslim is instructed to focus all his attention on that very name. Every Muslim, man or woman, has the ambition of dying with the sacred name of God on his or her lips. When the news of his death circulates, all Muslims who hear it spontaneously repeat the Quranic words: *Inna lillahi wa inna ilayhi raji'un* ('To God we belong, and to Him we return'). The funeral prayers, which are the last act of service to him, reverberate with the name of God from beginning to end. These prayers are a solemn request to the Almighty by the participants for the salvation of the soul of the departed, and for themselves to be granted a life of loyalty and devotion to Him in this world and of peace and felicity in the next. As the body is lowered into the grave, it is to the accompaniment of these words: "In the name of God, and according to the way and religion of His Apostle." In the grave, the face is turned towards that universal centre of divine worship and monotheism, the Kab'ah, or House of God. However a Muslim may be buried, his face will, without exception, be turned towards that same place, in Mecca in Arabia. After the burial, Muslim passers-by will usually recite the Fatihah[74] at his grave and pray for the remission of his sins and the deliverance of his soul. In short, the name of God and His remembrance are a constant companion of a Muslim's life from the cradle to the grave.

These are the more important moments in a person's earthly sojourn. Yet in his every day existence, a Muslim is also never far from remembering God. When a Muslim sits down to eat, he begins his meal with the name of God, and he ends it in the same manner. Those who are particular about observing the Sunnah of the Prophet carry out even the smallest tasks in life with the name of their Lord on their lips and an awareness of Him in their hearts. This is the case even for something as trifling as a sneeze; a Muslim is required to remember God when he lets it out, while those who hear it are instructed to respond with a prayer for him. Furthermore, the daily conversation of a Muslim is interspersed with phrases like *Ma sha Allah* (As God wills), *In sha Allah* (If God wills) and *La hawla wa la quwwata illa billah* (There is no power nor might except from God). These phrases, apart from being ideal prayer-formulas, have gained currency as terms of everyday speech, not only in Arabic, but in the languages of countries where Muslims have been living for some time and which have received the impress of Islamic Civilisation. In reality, these phrases are convenient aids to remembering God. The culture, language and daily life of no other people is so thoroughly steeped in a faith in God's existence and an all-embracing consciousness of Him. The basic ingredient of the culture and civilisation of Indian Muslims, regardless of race, nationality and geography, is this very faith and consciousness which has become the mark and symbol of their daily existence.

Monotheism

The second main constituent of Muslim culture is the creed of Monotheism. Belief in the oneness of God is manifest in all of their activities, from spiritual conviction to practical conduct and from worship to festivals and ceremonies. Five times a day it is proclaimed from the minarets of the mosques that no one is worthy of worship except the One God. Their homes and studios are expected to be free from every trace of idolatry and polytheism; photographs, statues and images having been prohibited for them by their religion. The same principle must be followed even while making or buying toys for children. Be it a religious or a national celebration, the birthday of a spiritual leader or a political hero, or the ceremony of national flag-hoisting, it is forbidden to bow before it or to pay it floral tributes in any form. Whenever Muslims are loyal to the Islamic Civilisation, they will remain strictly removed from such practices. Transgressing the limits of Monotheism while imitating the manners and customs of another people, even in such minor matters as giving a name, observing a ceremony, showing respect to elders, or expressing one's modesty and humility, is an act contrary to the spirit and teachings of Islam.

Human Dignity and Equality
The notion of human dignity and equality has become an essential part of the nature of Muslims and a permanent attribute of the Islamic character. Concepts such as social exclusiveness or untouchability are completely foreign to Muslim society. A Muslim will have no hesitation in dining with another Muslim or any other person. A group of Muslims will readily eat from the same vessel, eat the food left over by another, or drink the water remaining in his tumbler. Master and slave will stand in the same row for prayer, standing shoulder to shoulder with each other. Any learned person, however lowly he may be, socially or economically, can lead the prayer and the highest dignitaries and noblemen will follow him readily.

Lesser Attributes
Besides these fundamental characteristics, there are some other distinguishing features of this Abrahamic Civilisation that are of lesser importance and which are common to Muslims everywhere. These include habits and customs, such as performing all good deeds with the right hand, for example eating, drinking and passing something to someone. Another example is certain clothing-restrictions. For instance, clothes must cover the body properly, the lower garment must be long enough to conceal the knees but not so long as to go beyond the ankles; men are forbidden to wear silk; and there is also an emphasis on cleanliness. Adherence to these regulations will generally be the rule where Islamic Civilisation is present in its true, unpolluted form, and

where this is not the case, this is generally a sign of social and moral degeneration.

Fine Arts

Simplicity and sobriety are other characteristics of the Islamic Civilisation. In the matter of fine arts, it adopts a balanced temperate attitude. It does appreciate beauty and refinement, yet, at the same time, it frowns heavily upon certain forms of self-indulgence and sensuality to which the West has given the imposing label of "Fine Arts". Some of these are dancing, painting and photography (of living beings), and sculpture. Similarly, there are certain things in which Islam has advised caution and moderation. For instance, a Muslim is permitted to enjoy music, but within certain limits. Absorption in fine arts is, in any case, contrary to the spirit and social aims of Islamic Civilisation, while being inimical to being conscious of God and concerned about the Hereafter, as well as to the high ethical standards expected of a Muslim. Had the check and control of the Islamic Sharia and Civilisation not been there, it would not have been possible for Indian Muslims to maintain the temperateness that is their distinction, to varying extents, in a country that, from ancient times, has been so strongly attached to fine arts that they have become a part of popular worship.

Islamic Morality

Among the moral attributes that have particularly influenced Islamic culture are hospitality, liberality and open-handedness. These qualities are part of the legacy of the Prophet Ibrahim about whose generous reception of guests there occurs the following verse in the Quran: "Has the story reached thee of the honoured guests of Ibrahim?" (51:24).

Pilgrims and foreign chroniclers who had the occasion to live, for any length of time, among communities tracing their descent from him – either racially or spiritually – have recorded most pleasant memories of their stay in this regard. They have been invariably impressed by the warm hospitality and friendliness that these communities customarily afford guests and strangers. One can still notice in Middle Eastern countries that have not yet been overwhelmed by the mounting tide of Western Civilisation glimpses of the hospitality that enabled globetrotters like Ibn Battuta and Ibn Jubayr to enjoy the comfort and warmth of home during their travels. The Indian Muslims, despite being so far away from the natural seat of Islamic Civilisation and despite the fact that Islam reached their country long after it had passed the peak of its glory, are also conspicuous for their cordial treatment of their guests. Hospitality is a part of the tradition of Muslim homes, and although modern economic conditions have put a curb on it, Muslims still feel happy on the arrival of a guest and consider it a source of good fortune and an Islamic virtue to entertain them openheartedly.

Indian Influences
One of the most valuable fruits of the Indo-Islamic fusion is the Urdu language. Refined and progressive to its very core, this language represents what is best in the Arabic, Persian, Turkish and Sanskrit languages.

The dress of the upper and urban sections of Indian Muslims is another noteworthy example of the intermingling of Indian and Islamic cultures. It reflects refinement of taste and polished living in good measure. Furthermore, there is the graceful, easy and well-mannered mode of life which developed in Delhi, Hyderabad and the other important centres of Muslim influence towards the end of the Mughal rule.

An intense respect for parents, including displaying a particular level of humility and proper behaviour in their presence, and the exaggerated purdah of women along with certain other special regulations governing their conduct, are features which are not generally found among Muslims of other lands. In their evolution, the peculiar conditions of life in India, the needs and interests of Muslims as the ruling race and indigenous customs and traditions have all played a role.

The practice so commonly observed among Indian Muslims of marrying only from within the family, from a particular group of families or from a family of equal genealogical status is also typically Indian and influenced wholly by the caste system and other distinctions of birth prevalent in the country. Muslims living outside India look upon such customs with curiosity. They are not bound by them and, when contracting marriage, only give thought to social and economic considerations, as well as, of course, to personal inclination. Similarly, the custom of making excessive fuss on occasions of joy or grief, for example by spending beyond their means and displaying unnecessary ostentation, is a particularity of Indian society which has established itself amongst Muslims. In reality, the correct Islamic manner of carrying out such ceremonies is to display simplicity and quiet dignity.

The disgraceful treatment of servants by their masters, which was sometimes so outrageous as to reduce the servants to the level of untouchables, is again a product of the social norms adopted from India together with being a mark of the general degeneration that had set in amongst Muslims during the declining years of their power.

However, when all is said and done, it is an incontrovertible fact that Muslims have benefited from the ancient cultural heritage of India and been enriched by it in several ways. Their ability to successfully meet the onslaught of Western Civilisation and preserve their own cultural identity, something that has not been possible in the so-called Islamic countries, and the depth and profundity of their thought and mysticism (*Tasawwuf*) are due largely to the social, cultural and intellectual background of India. This background, in conjunction with Islam's basic inclinations and way of life, have given shape to a composite Indo-Islamic culture, merging the supranational Islamic Civilisation with the local philosophy and social design of India.

Despite this, Islamic values and ethical standards have suffered a distinct transformation in India. Although much less than that experienced by other peoples who, like Muslims, came from alien lands to make India their home, this was still profound enough to move a sensitive and well-meaning Muslim poet of the 19th century, Khwaja Altaf Husain, to make a friendly complaint about it to the Motherland.[76] When two civilisations meet, the transmission of cultural influences and impulses is always a two-way process. One of them cannot influence the other without simultaneously being influenced by it. Such a thing would be wrong and unnatural. Human existence is based essentially on the noble principle of give-and-take. In it lies its strength and glory.

Chapter 6

Some Special Features of The Medieval Educational System

The medieval education system was not without its faults. Both technically and academically, it suffered from a number of defects and shortcomings. However, the glowing religious fervour of its architects and other leading men equipped it with certain values that are not found in modern educational systems. Here we aim to summarise some of these values, although the following examples offer only a few of the innumerable instances of lofty idealism and religious zeal one comes across when examining the educational history of India under the Muslims.

Sincerity and Self-Denial

Utter sincerity and self-effacement were the main distinguishing characteristics of the teachers of old. They believed, as a matter of faith, in the religious merit of the profession of teaching and the reward promised for it in the Hereafter. As a result, most, if not all teachers looked upon their work as an act of worship and a religious duty, seeking God's good pleasure thereby. Many of them lived like ascetics, enduring poverty with forbearance and good cheer. Remarkable instances of this can be found in the records of the lives of Muslim ulema and teachers from those times.

For example, Maulana Ghulam Ali Azad Bilgrami relates about the well-known teacher and mentor Mir Tufail Muhammad Bilgrami, Mir Syed Mubarak that:

> "One day I was with Mir Mubarak when he rose to perform the *wudu*,[76] but staggered and fell down. I rushed to his aid and lifted him up. It took him some time to regain consciousness; then I enquired about his condition. After great persuasion he told me that he had eaten nothing for the last three days. The Maulana had not revealed his situation to anyone, nor accepted anything from anybody during that time. I was moved to tears on hearing it and returned home at once. I prepared the Maulana's favourite dish and took it to him. The Maulana expressed great pleasure at it; he bestowed much affection on me and blessed me profusely, but then he said, "If you do not mind, may I say something?" I begged him to do so, whereupon he observed, "Such a food is known among us, the Sufis, as *Ta'am-i-Ishraf*,[77] and although the *fiqh* does not prohibit it – the Sharia even allows the eating of impure food after three days of continuous starvation – it is against the practice of Sufi-ascetics to avail themselves of *Ta'am-i-Ishraf*."
>
> After this I quickly left the place taking the food back with me. I waited outside for some time, then went in again and asked the Maulana, "Were you expecting me to bring back the meal after I had taken it away?" "No" the Maulana replied. "Then it has ceased to be *Ta'am-i-Ishraf* now." I said. "You were not look-

Some Special Features of The Medieval Educational System

ward to it." My argument appealed to the Maulana and he agreed to eat. He remarked, "You have acted very wisely today".[78]

Admittedly, this is a unique case, but the educational history of medieval India is replete with glittering examples of ascetic self-denial and devotion to learning as a high religious duty. So much so that these qualities seem to have become part of the educational set-up during those days. No less astonishing is the following example of sincerity and self-denial on the part of teachers from the same period.

Maulana Abdul Rahim (d. 1884) was a teacher in Rampur. The Commissioner of Rohilkhand, Mr Hawkins, offered him the post of teacher in Bareilly College with a salary of 2501 rupees per month with a promise of a further pay rise in the future. The Maulana declined the offer, pleading that he would thereby forfeit the monthly stipend of 10 rupees he was getting from the Rampur State. Taken by surprise at this reply, the Commissioner enquired why the Maulana should bother about the stipend when he was offering him twenty-five times as much. The Maulana then said that there was a jujube tree in the courtyard of his house in Rampur with the sweetest fruit, and he would sorely miss it if he moved to Bareilly. The materialistic Englishman could still not understand the Maulana's excuse, and explained that the jujubes could easily be brought to Bareilly from Rampur for the Maulana to enjoy. The Maulana then put forward another argument, saying that his pupils in Rampur would be at great loss if he moved to Bareilly, while he too would be deprived of the opportunity of serving them. The Commissioner replied that he would grant them scholarships to complete their education at Bareilly. The Maulana then played his last card. He asked what he could say to God on the Day of Judgment for accepting remuneration for the sacred work of teaching. The Englishman then gave up in desperation and the Maulana spent the rest of his days in Rampur on a stipend of 10 rupees a month.[79]

Devotion to Work
The teachers of bygone days were so thoroughly devoted to their work that it is impossible to properly convey it today without the aid of examples. They made the work of teaching and instruction the sole passion of their lives and engaged themselves in it during most of the hours of the day and night right up until the end of their lives.

Allama Wajihuddin Gujarati, for instance, taught regularly for 60 to 65 years. Maulana Abdus Salam Lahori, Mulla Abdul Hakim Sialkoti and Maulana Ali Asghar Kannauji did so for 60 years, and Maulana Ahmad Amethwi, known as Mulla Jiwan, until the very last day of his life. It is said of some teachers that they used to give lessons even while eating or going out somewhere. Mulla Abdul Qadir Badayuni said of his teacher, Maulana Abdullah Badayuni, that: "A party of pupils used to accompany him when he went to the market to buy provisions for his family, and the Maulana would teach them on the way."[80]

Maulana Abdul Hayy Lucknawi Firangi Mahali, an outstanding scholar of the latter period, regularly gave a lesson before the Fajr (early morning) prayer. Many other teachers of the past are known to have done the same.

Devotion to Pupils
The deep and sincere affection teachers of the past had for their pupils now appears to be the stuff of legends. They literally treated them as their own children, and they would often bear their expenses and share their meals with them. For example, it is recorded that the famous teacher and royal physician to the court of Akbar, Hakim Ali Gilani "regularly gave lessons to students and never took his meals without them."[81]

Maulana Muhammad Afzal was so strongly attached to his pupils that, when his pupil Mulla Mahmud Jaunpuri died, the shock of it proved too much for him. Maulana Ghulam Ali Azad Bilgrami writes: "No one saw the Maulana smile (after it), until after forty days he himself went up to join his pupil."[82]

Maulana Abdul Ali Bahrul Uloom was invited to Rohal (Burdwan) on a sizeable salary by Munshi Sadruddin. The Maulana pointed out that there were about a hundred students with him, and it was not possible for him to accept the offer unless adequate provision was also made for their boarding and lodging. It was only after Munshi Sadruddin had agreed to this condition that the Maulana went. Similarly, when the Maulana took up service in Madras at the invitation of Nawab Walajah, he used to spend his entire salary of 1,000 rupees a month on his students and no part of it would reach his family at Firangi Mahal in Lucknow. Worried, his son, Maulana Abdul Nafey, went to Madras to plead with him to send some part of his income for the maintenance of his dependents, but the Maulana remained adamant.[83]

Attachment of Students to Teachers

For their part, the students were bound to their teachers by the strongest ties of devotion, reverence and loyalty. On hearing the report of the death of Mulla Nizamuddin of Firangi Mahal (which later turned out to be false), one of his pupils, Syed Kamaluddin Azimabadi, died of shock, while another, Syed Zarif Azimabadi, cried so hard that his eyes were permanently damaged.[84] Even if these incidents are exceptions, the incredible devotion of pupils to their teachers was a common feature of the educational system, as we learn from the records left behind by scholars about their masters.

Patronage by Kings and Noblemen

Kings and noblemen vied with each other in their patronage of learned scholars and teachers. They considered it a privilege and a religious obligation to serve men of arts and learning and provide for their needs and comfort. The following incident narrated by Muhammad Qasim Bijapuri in his *Tarikh-i-Ferishta* illustrates this point:

> "Once Qadi Shihabuddin Daulatabadi was gravely ill. Sultan Ibrahim Sharqi went to visit him, and after enquiring about his condition, making proper arrangements for his treatment and looking into other necessary things, he asked for a cup of water. When it was brought, the Sultan made a circular movement with the cup around the Maulana's head in token of an offering, and then drank the water, praying, 'O God! Send down on me the affliction ordained for the Maulana and grant him recovery.'"[85]

On the death of Amir Fathullah Shirazi, Emperor Akbar is reported to have expressed his grief in these words:

> "Had the enemy taken him prisoner and demanded the whole of my Empire's treasure as ransom, the bargain would still have been a most profitable one; the precious gem would not have proved costly at that price."

Mulla Abdul Hakim Sialkoti was weighed twice in silver and Qadi Muhammad Aslam Harawi (father of Allama Mir Zahid) once in gold by Emperor Shah Jahan, this being the highest form of recognition possible.

The staggering reception Maulana Bahrul Uloom was accorded at Madras has been described by Maulana Waliullah

Some Special Features of The Medieval Educational System

Firangi Mahali:

> "When his palanquin reached the royal palace the Maulana wanted to step down from it, but Nawab Walajah motioned him to remain seated, and, applying his own shoulder to the palanquin, he carried it in. The Nawab, then, urged the Maulana to sit in his place on the throne; he kissed his feet, and said, 'I never knew that my stars were so blessed that you would grace me with a visit and shed lustre on my house by your presence.'"[86]

Due to the magnanimity and encouragement of generous rulers and other wealthy individuals, a vast network of madrasahs was set up in the country. We can deduce the situation in the rest of the country from the following account by Maulana Ghulam Ali Azad Bilgrami of the incredible expansion of education through private patronage in his own province of Oudh:

> "Throughout the Province of Oudh, as also in the Province of Allahabad, there are found, at every five or, at the most, ten miles, settlements of respectable and high ranking (Muslim) families. These families enjoy pensions or fees in land or cash granted to them by the Government for their maintenance. They have built mosques, schools and spiritual seminaries from place to place, where teachers and learned men are actively engaged in the spread of education. They have produced a great urge among the people for the pursuit of knowledge. Students in large numbers travel from one town to another in search of learning and take up their residence where they find the greatest scope for undertaking their studies. Their needs are

taken care of by benevolent individuals who regard it an act of great virtue. Emperor Shah Jahan often used to say, 'The eastern areas are the Shiraz of my Empire.'"[87]

Concern for Spiritual Advancement

With all their intellectual and literary attainments and importance, the learned scholars of old were fully aware of their spiritual needs and strove hard to purify themselves and to cultivate a living, all-pervading consciousness of the Almighty. They believed that it was as necessary for their fulfilment to respectfully serve spiritual guides and mentors as to sit at the feet of secular teachers to acquire temporal knowledge and learning. They did not allow any consideration of prestige to stand in their way. They zealously upheld their honour and dignity before worldly kings and peers and did not bend even an inch in obedience to them, and yet they were the epitome of submissiveness and humility when it came to the spiritual masters. The unique combination of self-awareness and self-denial was a striking characteristic of the lives of the teachers of that era. It is an incontrovertible fact that the outstanding personalities in the educational history of medieval India were all unfailingly bound in allegiance and loyalty to some spiritual leader of their time.

During its initial stage, the entire educational and intellectual structure of India bore the impress of three spiritual masters, Abdul Muqtadir Kindi Thanesari (d. 1388) and his two pupils, Maulana Khwaja Dehlavi (d. 1406) and Shaykh Ahmad Thanesari (d. 1398). All of these were spiritual disciples of Shaykh Nasiruddin Chiragh-i-Dehli.

Then there was Wajihuddin ibn Nasrullah Gujarati (d. 1589), "who devoted 67 years of his life to teaching religious and secular sciences at Ahmedabad. His pupils were dispersed over a wide area, from Ahmedabad to Lahore, spreading light and learning wherever they were. He had the honour of being elevated to the rank of 'Master of Masters' during his own lifetime."[88]

The famous educational centres of Kora Jahanabad, Amethi, Jaunpur and Lucknow shone solely with his radiance. He himself was the spiritual protege of Shaykh Muhammad Ghaus Gwaliori and received numerous blessings from him. Two other notable scholars and teachers of the time, Shah Pir Muhammad and Maulana Ghulam Naqshband, themselves spiritual masters, belonged to this same line of spiritual guidance and instruction.

It was then the turn of Mulla Nizamuddin to dominate the educational scene from India to Iran and Afghanistan. He was not only a devoted follower of Qadiri saint Syed Abdul Razzaq Bansawi, but he was literally intoxicated with love for his mentor. Every word in his biographical study of him, *Manaqib-i-Razzaqia*, displays the depth and intensity of his devotion to him.

The founder of Darul Uloom Deoband with its nationwide activities in the fields of religious and spiritual guidance and reform, Maulana Muhammad Qasim Nanautawi (d. 1879) and its other patron and benefactor, Maulana Rashid Ahmad Gangohi (d. 1905) were the disciples and *khalifahs* of Hajji Imdadullah Mahajir Makki. Likewise, Maulana Syed Muhammad Ali Almongiri, who founded the Nadwatul Ulama at Lucknow, was a *khalifah* of Maulana Fazlur Rahman of Ganj Moradabad in the district of Unnao. Thus, at every turn of its history, we find the educational endeavour of the medieval era touched by the spiritual splendour of some saintly man of God. We believe the secret of its strength, effectiveness and spiritual glory lay in this.

Curiously enough, teachers and scholars of exceptional status and ability were often allied to spiritual masters who were not technically scholars themselves and were not even considered learned by their contemporaries. For example we can see the devoted attachment of Maulana Muhammad Ismail Shaheed and Maulana Abdul Hayy Burhanwi to Syed Ahmad Shaheed, of an outstanding genius like Mulla Nizamuddin to Syed Abdul Razzaq Bansawi, and of that great scholar with an original mind, Maulana Muhammad Qasim Nanautawi to Hajji Imdadullah. These instances, which cannot be ascribed to mere chance, are the clearest examples of the utter humility and total selflessness of the learned scholars of that time. They tell of the priceless intellectual and spiritual qualities that held the key to the phenomenal success they achieved in their mission. As we have already said, the combination of moral and spiritual evolution with intellectual glory, and of deep learning with earnestness and seeking closeness to God were the chief attributes of the older educational set-up. Consequently, an intimate relationship was forged between men of learning and enlightenment and the general public, which enabled the former to exert a strong and ennobling influence on society as a whole. Furthermore, the scholars and other learned men were generally able to summon up enough moral stamina to resist the pull of worldly temptations and the benefits that could be accrued from princely courts and save themselves from other moral weaknesses. This would not have been possible on the strength of intellect and learning alone. The single-minded devotion and the deep sincerity and selflessness, with which teachers and scholars continued to serve the cause of learning for as much as 800 years, were due, in no small measure, to the guidance, training, and moral and spiritual purification received at the hands of holy men.

Until the very end, it was a tradition with Arabic institutions that their students, after they had completed their studies, would go to live for some time with spiritual guides whom they, or their teachers, held in high regard and with whom they also felt themselves to be in tune spiritually. Here they would develop that aspect of their personality which could not be taken care of in a purely academic environment. The students coming out of the institution founded by Maulana Lutfullah during the latter period, sought the blessed company of Maulana Fazlur Rahman of Ganj Moradabad. As for the madrasahs of north-western India, like those of Deoband and Saharanpur, their teachers and pupils headed instead to Thana Bhawan, Gangoh and Raipur, where Hajji Imdadullah Mahajir Makki, Maulana Rashid Ahmad Gangohi and their disciples served as beacons of moral and spiritual guidance.

Chapter 7

Modern Religious, Cultural and Educational Centres of the Muslims

Darul Uloom Deoband

The failure of the uprising of 1857, headed by the Muslim religious leaders, produced an overwhelming sense of defeat and frustration amongst the Muslims of India. They quickly fell victim to a feeling of dejection and self-pity. Encouraged by the victory of the British army, Christian missionaries began to openly declare that India was a gift and a trust from Jesus, and it was now their duty to vigorously propagate Christianity there. The Muslims, on the other hand, were overcome by spiritual and moral weakness and became increasingly ignorant about their faith under the influence of western culture and education. It was feared that their future generations would be lost to Islam and that they would lose all connection with the Islamic Shariah, moral system and civilisation. For this reason, certain courageous and farsighted ulema realised the need to establish theological institutions which could keep alive the link of the rising Muslim generations with their faith and also be instrumental in the preservation and promotion of Islamic religious and moral knowledge. The Darul Uloom of

Deoband occupies a position of foremost importance among the Muslim religious institutions that were thus established.

Beginning in a modest way as an unpretentious madrasah, the Darul Uloom made steady progress thanks to the sincerity and dedication of its founders, patrons and teachers. It eventually blossomed into a big Islamic university, becoming the largest seat of Muslim religious learning in the whole of Asia.

It first opened in 1866 in a small mosque in the town of Deoband, Saharanpur, as a primary madrasah run by a local Muslim divine, known by the name of Hajji Muhammad Abid. For its magnificent progress and development, it is indebted mainly to the courage, fortitude and religious fervour of Maulana Muhammad Qasim Nanautawi, who was associated with the institution from the very beginning. In the later years of his life, the Maulana willingly devoted all his time and energy to its advancement. From its earliest days, the Darul Uloom has been extremely fortunate in enjoying the services and patronage of sincere workers and teachers, with the result that the spirit of piety, humility and selflessness has become a part of its very nature. Among its teachers of outstanding merit and sincerity, the names of Maulana Muhammad Yaqub Nanautawi, Shaykh-ul-Hind Maulana Mahmud-ul-Hasan, Mufti Azizur Rahman, Maulana Ghulam Rasul, Maulana Anwar Shah, Maulana Husayn Ahmad Madani, Maulana Syed Asghar Husayn and Maulana Aziz Ali will always be remembered. The range of its academic activities has been steadily expanded and its fame has travelled far and wide, as has that of its teachers for their deep learning, their moral and spiritual integrity, and their expertise in the sciences of Hadith and Islamic Jurisprudence. For this reason it has attracted students not only from all over India but from other, distant Islamic lands. It now caters for more than 1,500 students.

Over 10,000 young men have gone through its doors after completing their studies; half of them having done the course of Farigh al-Tahsil and attaining the highest degree in Islamic theology. Of these, about 500 students came from foreign lands, including Dagestan, Afghanistan, Kiev, Bukhara, Kazan, Russia, Azerbaijan, the tribal belt of the north-western regions of the Asian sub-continent, Turkey, Tibet, China, the islands of the Indian Ocean and Arabia. The benefits arising from the reformist endeavours of Deobandi ulema are evident in the religious life of Indian Muslims. These efforts have been particularly praiseworthy in the areas of rectifying religious beliefs and weeding out innovations, preaching and propagating Islam, and refuting false claims levelled against Islam by malicious critics through discussion and debate. Several Deobandi graduates have made their mark in politics. They were also in the vanguard of the struggle for freedom.

Unflinching loyalty to the faith, strict adherence to the Hanafi school of law, upholding the way of the pious predecessors and safeguarding the Sunnah of the Prophet can be said to be the major traits of the tradition of Darul Uloom Deoband.

Mazahir Uloom, Saharanpur

Another great religious institution in Saharanpur is the madrasah of Mazahir Uloom. It is second only to Darul Uloom Deoband in the number of its pupils and keenness for theological learning. Named after Maulana Muhammad Mazhar Nanautawi, its foundations were laid in 1866 by the blessed hands of Maulana Sa'adat Ali Saharanpuri. It had the privilege of enjoying, in succession, the patronage of Maulana Rashid Ahmad Gangohi, Maulana Khalil Ahmad Saharanpuri and Maulana Ashraf Ali Thanwi. Among its more eminent teachers were Maulana Sabit Ali, Maulana Inayat Elahi, Maulana Khalil Ahmad, Maulana Muhammad Yahiya, Maulana Abdul Latif, Maulana Muhammad Ilyas, Maulana Abdul Rahman, Shaykhul Hadeeth Maulana Muhammad Zakaria and Maulana Asadullah. With regard to its ideology, traditions and environment, Mazahir Uloom is very much akin to Darul Uloom Deoband. It has similarly produced a large number of qualified ulema and keen students of Islamic learning. Its scholars have admirably served the study of the Hadith, in particular, having produced valuable commentaries on several collections of the Prophet's hadith. Both its teachers and students have been famous for their austerity, contentment and righteous conduct.

Other Madrasahs of the Nizamiyyah Pattern
Besides these, there are several other madrasahs which follow the Nizamiyyah course of study[89] and are also like them in many other ways. They have played an admirable role in the promotion of Islamic theological learning and the general religious reform of Indian Muslims. Of these, the Shahi Madrasah of Moradabad and the Madrasa-i-Imdadia of Darbhanga are the most famous in northern India.

The Ahl-i-Hadith sect also has several of its own theological madrasahs, such as the Madrasa-i-Rahmania of Varanasi and the Madrasa-i-Ahmadiah Salafia, Lahria Sarai, Darbhanga. Its Madrasa-i-Rahmania at Delhi had to be closed after Partition in 1947, but the others are doing useful work.

Among the official and semi-official Arabic madrasahs, the Madrasa-i-'Alia of Rampur, Madrasa-i-'Alia of Calcutta and Madrasa-i-Shamsul Huda of Patna deserve special mention. At one stage, the madrasahs of Rampur and Calcutta were of great importance among the Muslim religious institutions of the land.

A number of madrasahs are also run by Shia Muslims, most of these being in their main religious and educational centre, Lucknow. The best known of the Shia madrasahs at Lucknow are Sultanul Madaris, Madrasa-i-Nazimia and Madrasatul Waizeen.

In the South, where there is considerable interest in religious education among Muslims, there are a large number of functioning Arabic madrasahs. More prominent among these are the

Madrasa-i-Nizamiya of Hyderabad, Jami'a-i-Darus-Salam of Osmanabad and al-Baqiyat us-Salehat of Vellore. The Madrasa-i-Jamalia of Madras was once a flourishing and progressive seat of Islamic instruction, but it became defunct some time ago. Attempts are now being made to revive it.

The region of Malabar (now a part of the state of Kerala) has always been known for its religious devoutness and attachment to the Arabic language. A large number of Arabic madrasahs are found there; those located in and around Calicut, such as Rauzatul Uloom, Madinatul Uloom and Sullam-us-Salam, are the most prominent. Here, the Arabic language ranks next in importance only to the state language (Malayalam) and to English and is taught in Muslim schools and colleges as the second language. The Kerala Government has even formulated an Arabic curriculum which is fairly successful. In Gujarat, there are many madrasahs of both the old and the modern style. The Jamia Islamia of Dabhel was once a very great institution, employing men of the calibre of Maulana Anwar Shah Kashmiri and Maulana Shabir Ahmad Osmani. Jami'a-i-Husainia and Jami'a-i-Ashrafia of Rander and the Arabic madrasahs of Chhapi and Anand are the most noteworthy.

Darul Uloom Nadwatul Ulama, Lucknow

Maulana Muhammad Ali of Monghyr would often debate with Christian missionaries. He also brought out a missionary and dialectical journal called, *Tuhfa-i-Muhammadiyah*. He was a man of vast knowledge and possessed a sharp mind. He realised that the traditional education system and the ancient scholastic theology could no longer achieve their intended goal. They were inadequate for combating the cultural influence of the West and producing preachers and scholars who could cope with the changing needs of the times. To achieve these aims, it was necessary to produce an improved and integrated syllabus, cutting short or amending the older, less relevant philosophical studies and incorporating the modern sciences.

This was a time when fierce controversies were raging among the various schools of Islamic jurisprudence – the Hanafi, the Shafi'i and the Ahl-i-Hadith – culminating in riots and legal action, to the general humiliation of the Muslims. The Maulana came to the conclusion that this dismal state of affairs could not be remedied until the qualities of broadmindedness and tolerance and the ability to rise above trivialities and disputations on details of *fiqh* could be developed among the teachers and scholars of Muslim religious institutions. He formed an association known as Nadwatul Ulama to reconcile the differences among the contending Muslim groups. Later, in 1898, he founded a model institution at Lucknow. Before long, the Darul Uloom Nadwatul Ulama succeeded in gaining the support and goodwill of concerned, broadminded ulema and opinion makers representing the different schools of thought, who voluntarily offered their services in various capacities. The names of Maulana Shilbi Nomani, Maulana Habibur Rahman Khan Sherwani, Maulana Abdul Haqq Haqqani, Maulana Shah Sulaiman Phulwarawi, Munshi Athar Ali Kakorwi, Munshi Ehtisham Ali Kakorwi, Maulana Muhammad Ibrahim Aarwi, Qadi Muhammad Sulaiman Mansurpuri, Maulana Sanaullah Amritsari, Maulana Sir Rahim Bakhsh, Maulana Masihuzzaman Khan (teacher of the late Mir Mahbub Ali Khan, the Nizam of Hyderabad), Maulana Khalilur Rahman Saharanpuri (son of Maulana Ahmad Ali Muhaddis), Maulana Hakim Syed Abdul Hayy, Nawab Syed Ali Hasan Khan (son of Nawab Siddiq Hasan Khan of Bhopal) and Maulana Hakim Dr Syed Abdul Ali deserve especially to be put on record in this regard.

Ignoring the view of the older madrasahs that to depart in the slightest from the ancient style of learning was a transgression and a sin, and of the modern universities that apart from modern knowledge, everything in the domain of learning was worthless,

Nadwatul Ulama was planned from the beginning to pursue a balanced and moderate course. Its founders were suspicious of extremism, both ancient and modern, and considered the intellectual and social exclusiveness and rigidity of the ulema, their juristic arguing and detailed disputations as highly detrimental to Islam and the Muslims.

Nadwatul Ulama was thus designed to strive towards a synthesis of the old and the new. Its sponsors believed that the Islamic faith itself was unequivocally eternal and absolute, and would permit no alteration, but that knowledge was evolutionary and changing. The lofty objective of the institution was to bring together the various sects of Ahl al-Sunnah into a single unity. It did not subscribe to the view that the Islamic theological sciences or teaching syllabus were sacrosanct and unalterable.

Nadwatul Ulama focused its attention primarily on the teaching of the Quran as an eternal program of life. It also took up the teaching of Arabic as a living language since this held the key to understanding the Quran. It did not commit the folly, as was generally the case in India, of regarding Arabic as a dead classical language that was no longer current and in everyday use anywhere in the world. It excluded from its curriculum, or reduced the importance of such sciences as had ceased to be of real value in the modern era, and in their place it introduced those modern branches of study that were essential for the ulema to render an effective service to Islam in the prevailing context.

Another one of its main aims was to produce preachers and interpreters who could present Islam to the modern world in a bold and effective manner and in a form and language it could understand. By the grace of God, it has achieved admirable success in accomplishing these aims. It has produced exemplary servants of Islam and high-ranking scholars who can be held up as role models for the world of Islam. These scholars have made invaluable contributions to the study of Islamic history, literature, scholastic theology and the biography of the Prophet.

Madrasatul Islah, Sarai Mir
Madrasatul Islah was started by Maulana Hameeduddin Farahi at Sarai Mir in Azamgarh in 1909, along the lines of Nadwatul Ulama, Lucknow. The subject of special study here has been the commentary of the Holy Quran. Its teachers and pupils have faithfully followed the path trod by Maulana Farahi in his own commentary of the Quran. It is noted for austerity and for its outstanding academic atmosphere.

Darul Uloom Bhopal
Bhopal has historically been an important seat of Muslim theological learning. However, after the merger of Indian states following India's independence in 1947, it was feared that religious learning would come to an end, not only in Bhopal but in the whole of central India (now called Madhya Pradesh). This fear was dispelled by the prompt action taken by certain ulema of vision and courage. Under the patronage of Syed Sulaiman Nadwi, then the Qadi of the state and Rector of Jami'a Ahmadiyah at Bhopal. and the ceaseless endeavours of Maulana Muhammad Imran Khan Nadwi, a madrasah called Darul Uloom was founded in the spacious Taj-ul-Masajid mosque in Bhopal. It was modelled after the Nadwatul Ulama of Lucknow so far as the course of studies and method of instruction were concerned. It is currently functioning admirably under the leadership of Maulana Muhammad Imran Khan Nadwi and has risen, within a few years, to being one of the foremost Muslim theological institution of Madhya Pradesh.

Modern Institutions
In addition to Arabic madrasahs, there are also universities founded by Muslims at Aligarh, Delhi[90] and Hyderabad that offer the Muslim youth the opportunity to study modern subjects and

foreign languages and train them so they too can work in public services and participate fully in all national activities.

Muslim University, Aligarh

The oldest and the most famous of these universities is the Muslim University of Aligarh. This university has had a powerful influence on shaping the mental attitude, collective character and the politics of modern Indian Muslims and is one of the biggest seats of learning in the country. It was founded by Sir Syed Ahmad Khan in 1875, when it was called Madrasatul Uloom or the Muhammadan Anglo-Oriental College.

A lamentable intellectual and social decay afflicted the Muslims following the Upheaval of 1857, and they became acutely despondent and frustrated. The British rulers severely mistrusted them and looked upon them with suspicion and contempt. As a result, they became almost totally barred from all public positions. Until that time, they were the ruling race and the arbiters of India's destiny; now they were completely ejected from its government and administration.

Sir Syed was blessed by God with an awakened heart and a sympathetic soul. He had seen the twilight of Muslim power in India. When night finally descended on the Muslims it stirred him powerfully and he made earnest efforts to bring about their recovery and rehabilitation. He came to the conclusion that, as long as Muslims did not receive an English education and adopt the western mode of living, they would not be able to shed the inferiority complex they had so mournfully acquired; nor would the British masters be willing to treat them with equality. It was with these aims in mind that he established a college at Aligarh, which in 1921 attained the status of a university.

The Muslim University was highly successful in its aims, and in no time at all gained the confidence of the British Government. Students from well-to-do Muslim families were attracted to it in ever-increasing numbers, and after completing their education they were appointed to the highest offices of the state that were open to Indians. The University also played an important role in the political life of the country, particularly of the Muslims. It is here that the movement for a separate Muslim homeland, as against the ideal of a united Indian nation, was born. Not only has it successfully preserved its denomination and many of its basic traditions in the post-freedom days, but it has also developed and progressed in several ways. Its annual expenditure has now reached 41 million rupees and it caters for about 10,000 students, forty percent of which are Hindus. The standard of discipline there has generally been higher than in other universities. The number of Hindu students in the faculties of Medicine and Engineering are approximately sixty-five per cent and fifty-five percent respectively.

Jami'a Millia, Delhi
During the hectic days of the Khilafat agitation, a number of outstanding alumni of the Muslim University lost faith in it and in 1920 founded an independent national university under the title: Jami'a Millia. Its foundation-stone was laid by the highly revered Shaykh-ul-Hind Maulana Mahmud Hasan Deobandi. A few years later, the new university moved to Delhi. The chief architect of the idea of a national university was Maulana Muhammad Ali, who was aided by his well-known colleagues, Hakim Ajmal Khan and Dr Mukhtar Ahmad Ansari. The Jami'a had on its staff men whose sole ambition was to serve the nation. Having chosen for themselves a life of trial and hardship, they valiantly withstood many difficulties under the inspiring leadership of the renowned educationist, the late Dr Zakir Husain Khan, the former President of India. The Jami'a holds a brilliant record of work in promoting learning and culture. It is now a flourishing institution under the generous patronage of the Government of India and

the able guidance of its Vice-Chancellor, Professor Masud Hasan.

Jami'a Osmania, Hyderabad

The most remarkable feature of Jami'a Osmania, Hyderabad was that the medium of instruction was Urdu. For this purpose, a vast storehouse of knowledge, covering all subjects, was translated under its aegis from foreign languages into Urdu. It also took on the extremely useful work of coining Urdu equivalents for technical and literary terms. Thus, Osmania University has been of great benefit in developing the Urdu language. Some of the best teachers and educationists of the land have served on its staff,[91] and even now, after all the revolutionary changes that have taken place since independence, especially in that part of India, it has managed to preserve some of its old characteristics.

Intermediate and Degree Colleges

Muslims have also opened numerous Islamic Colleges that follow the officially prescribed curriculum but with certain suitable additions. There is at least one Muslim intermediate or degree college in all the important towns of northern India, while in the south there are a number of such institutions flourishing in the states of Madras and Kerala. Of these, the New College of Madras, the Jamal Muhammad College of Trichinopoly, the Osmania College of Kurnool and the Farooq College of Calicut are the best known.

Darul Musannifin, Azamgarh

A literary academy, called Darul Musannifin, was formed by Maulana Shibli Nomani at Azamgarh in 1914. It was its good fortune to function for over a quarter of a century under the distinguished guidance of Maulana Syed Sulaiman Nadwi. By 1960, fellows of this academy had produced some ninety books on various topics relating to religion, literature and history. No library worth its name in the country is today without the books produced by this academy. It still publishes a standard monthly journal, Ma'arif, under the editorship of Maulana Abdus Salam Qidwai and Syed Sabahuddin Abdul Rahman.

Nadwatul Musannifin, Delhi
A similar institution is Nadwatul Musannifin in Delhi. It was founded in 1938 and has so far (i.e. until 1960) produced eighty-eight noteworthy works of research on cultural and historical subjects. It also publishes a monthly literary magazine called Burhan, with Maulana Saeed Ahmad Akbarabadi as editor.

Majlis-i-Tahqiqat-o-Nashriyat-i-Islam, Lucknow
Another body of scholars and writers has recently been formed in Lucknow, under the name of Majlis-i-Tahqiqat-o-Nashriyat-i-Islam (Academy of Islamic Research and Publications). It aims to produce Islamic literature to meet the needs of both educated Muslims and non-Muslims. It has published a number of fine books within the couple of years since its establishment.

Muslim Educational Conference, Aligarh
The Muslim Educational Conference is the oldest educational association of Indian Muslims. It was founded by Sir Syed Ahmad Khan in 1886 to promote education amongst Muslims. The Conference has performed remarkable services in engendering Muslim political and educational awakening in the country. It was under its wings that the Muslim League was born in 1906; however, since 1947 it has sadly almost been a dead organisation. In the past its secretaries included men of the renown of Sir Syed Ahmad Khan, Nawab Waqar-ul-Mulk and Nawab Sadar Yar Jung Maulana Habibur Rahman Khan Sherwani.

Dini Talimi Board & Dini Talimi Council

India has chosen to be a secular state, to follow the Indian Constitution, not to discriminate between one community and another, and to guarantee the rights of citizenship to all citizens alike. However, the curriculum prescribed for schools in certain states conflicts with the basic ideals of Islam and poses a serious threat to the religious future of Muslims. To combat this danger and to safeguard the general interests of Muslims as a religious community, two organisations have recently been formed. These are the Dini Talimi Board (Muslim Religious Education Board) and the Dini Talimi Council (Muslim Religious Education Council), Uttar Pradesh. The former lies under the auspices of Jami'at-i-Ulema-i-Hind and the latter under representatives of the various sections of Muslim opinion in Uttar Pradesh. Both are doing useful work in their respective spheres of influence and madrasahs are being set up by them where Muslim children can receive instruction in Islamic theology and Urdu.

Dairatul Ma'arif, Hyderabad

The Dairatul Ma'arif of Hyderabad has enjoyed great prominence among the higher literary institutions of India. It was founded in 1888 through the determined efforts of Imad-ul-Mulk Syed Husain Bilgrami, Mulla Abdul Qaiyum and Fazeelat Jung Maulana Anwar Ullah Khan (the teacher of Mir Osman Ali Khan, the former Nizam of Hyderabad). The main purpose for establishing it was to unearth and publish rare manuscripts of literary and religious significance that were lying buried and forgotten in the ancient libraries and private collections of India. So far it has published over 150 priceless works on Hadith, Asma al-Rajal,[92] history, mathematics and philosophy. These books had long been forgotten in India and the wider Muslim World or existed as mere names in the minds of scholars and learned men. It is to the lasting credit of Dairatul Ma'arif that it has brought them into the public domain for the first time, and enabled researchers and scholars to derive full benefit from them. It is an achievement of which any literary institution can legitimately be proud.[93]

The services of Dairatul Ma'arif have been recognised by distinguished scholars in both the East and the West. In 1937, a party of teachers from the University of al-Azhar, Egypt, visited India on a tour. Its leader, Shaykh Ibrahim al-Jibali, expressed his appreciation of the activities of Dairatul M'aarif in the following words:

> "We greatly admire the efforts the Dairatul Ma'arif of Hyderabad is making towards the promotion of Islamic learning and culture. The ambitious men of the Daira have not only succeeded in discovering a large number of books by classical writers that were lying in obscurity or had been given up as untraceable but whose names were still ringing in the ears and for which minds were still yearning to profit by them, but they have also only published them after properly verifying, correcting, annotating and editing them. They have spared neither money nor pains. They have cared nothing for the hardships of the long journeys they had to undertake in seeking manuscripts nor for the great industry and mental labour involved in copying, checking and verifying them."[94]

Darul Tarjuma (now defunct), Hyderabad
When the Osmania University of Hyderabad adopted Urdu as its medium of instruction, the need was felt for a bureau of translation to transfer the standard works on the different subjects of study into Urdu. This led to the establishment of Darul Tarjuma in 1917. Translations of 358 books, in all, on History, Geography, Politics, Economics, Sociology, Logic, Philosophy, Metaphysics, Ethics, Psychology, Mathematics, Physics, Chemistry, Biology,

Medicine and Engineering were successfully undertaken.

The bureau was also charged with the work of converting modern technical terms into Urdu. This has been of immense benefit to the intellectual and literary circles of the country.

Among the writers and scholars who were associated with Darul Tarjuma were Dr Abdul Haqq, Maulana Abdul Majid Daryabadi, Abdullah al-Emadi, Molvi Wahiduddin Saleem Panipati, Molvi Inayatullah Dehlavi, Molvi Masud Ali Nadwi and Qadi Talammuz Husayn Gorakhpuri.

The annual expenditure of the bureau in 1948 was 261,415 rupees. It was abolished after the merger of Hyderabad, and its huge library containing books and manuscripts worth tens of millions of rupees was destroyed by fire.

Jami'at-i-Islami's Institution at Rampur

The Jami'at-i-Islami (Hind) has played a commendable role in producing Islamic literature. Its most praiseworthy contribution has been the preparation of a religiously-inspired course of study and textbooks for Muslim children in Urdu and Hindi. It is also running a model educational institution in Rampur.

Old Libraries

The keen interest shown by Muslims for learning during the days of their ascendancy can be seen from some of the libraries they built which have withstood the ravages of time. These libraries are also a universally accepted source of India's intellectual glory.

Muslim rulers, noblemen and scholars paid great attention to the establishment of good, first-class libraries with the result that a vast number of them were established in various places. At present, the biggest Muslim library is the Khuda Bux Library of Bankipur, Patna. This library is a huge treasure-house of rare books, including some of the oldest and most unique documents and manuscripts of universally celebrated books. The Raza Library of Rampur, the Kutub Khana-i-Asafia and the Sir Salar Jung Museum of Hyderabad, the Library of Nawab Sadar Yar Maulana Habibur Rahman Sherwani (Hyderabad), the Nadwa Library of Lucknow, the Library of Darul Uloom Deoband, the Azad Library of Aligarh, and the Library of Nasir-ul-Millet Maulana Nasir Husayn at Lucknow are some of the other more important Muslim libraries.

Scholars from both Islamic and Western countries are regularly drawn to these libraries. A delegation was sent to India by the Arab League in 1952 to make microfilm copies of priceless books for its international library, books that could be found nowhere else in the world. The delegation travelled throughout the country and copied onto microfilm hundreds of old and rare Arabic books preserved in the Muslim libraries of Lucknow, Rampur, Hyderabad, Aligarh, Tonk, Azamgarh, Calcutta Patna, and other places.

Chapter 8

The Role of Muslims in The Struggle for Freedom

Muslims at the Forefront
Muslims were at the forefront of the national struggle for freedom. After all, it was from their hands that the British had wrested power in India. As British imperialism was spreading over the country, devouring one province after the other, the first man to realise the gravity of the danger was the lionhearted Tipu Sultan of Mysore. He saw clearly that, unless determined efforts were made to thwart the nefarious designs of the greedy foreigners, they would swallow up the whole of India. With strong resolve, he unsheathed his sword and jumped into a fierce, life-and-death struggle against the British exploiters.

Tipu Sultan's Crusade
Tipu Sultan made a valiant bid to unite the Indian princes against the British usurpers. He even wrote to Sultan Salim III of Turkey, asking him to join hands with him to expel the British. His whole life was spent in this struggle, and he very nearly succeeded. The English were on the verge of being swept out of India when they

managed to achieve through diplomacy what they could not gain by arms. They cleverly obtained the support of some of the rulers from the south and by means of treachery and deceit brought to nought the patriotic ambitions of that gallant son of Mysore.

Tipu Sultan was finally killed in the thick of battle on 4th May 1799, preferring death to a life of servitude under the British. His famous, historic words, spoken a little before he met his death, were: "To live for a day like a tiger is far more precious than to live for a hundred years like a jackal."

It is reported that when the British Commander, General Harris, received the news of the Sultan's death and went to inspect his corpse, he cried out in exultation: "From today, India is ours." The history of India does not tell of a braver patriot and a more uncompromising enemy of foreign rule than him. In his lifetime he was the most hated man among the English. Out of spite, Englishmen in India even went as far as giving their dogs the name Tipu, and they continued to do so for a long time.[95]

The War of Independence

In May 1857, the Indian sepoys rose in open revolt against the oppressive misdeeds of their British masters, the contemptuous treatment meted out by them to their Indian subordinates and their insatiable lust for money and persistent violation of the religious sentiments of Hindus and Muslims. The sepoy uprising quickly developed into a national war with Hindus and Muslims fighting shoulder to shoulder for the emancipation of the Motherland. The rebels marched towards Delhi, the seat of the last of the Mughal Emperors, Bahadur Shah Zafar, and proclaimed him to be the spearhead of their struggle and symbol of national resistance. Battles were fought all over India under his flag. He was the unanimous choice of the people and their rightful leader and ruler, and Delhi was the nerve-centre of this patriotic India.[96]

Muslim Leadership during the War of Independence

Although the War of Independence was truly a national war in which Hindus and Muslims had participated freely and equally and India had not yet seen a more stirring spectacle of popular enthusiasm, unity and patriotism, its leadership was predominantly in the hands of Muslims. More often than not, the leaders of the movement, at various levels belonged to the Muslim Community.[97]

The Vengeance of the British

After the failure of the movement, for reasons that are well known, the British took savage revenge against the Indians and let loose a spate of fury that evokes memories of Genghis Khan and Hulagu Khan.[98] The rebels were ruthlessly pursued, caught and punished. There was ruin and desolation everywhere. The three young sons of the Emperor, to whom the British themselves had given asylum, were killed by them so ruthlessly that it made even the British shudder. Thirty-three other members of the imperial family, including the old and the infirm, were slain along with them.[99] The aging Emperor himself was humiliated in the most severe manner. He was tried for treason in excessively degrading circumstances and would have certainly been put to death had a high English army officer not guaranteed the security of his life. He was exiled to Burma to spend the rest of his days in utter poverty and indigence.

Death and Desolation

As the victorious British army entered the city of Delhi the terrible havoc they wreaked was like a confirmation of the Quranic verse:

> Kings, when they enter a country, despoil it and make the noblest of its people the meanest: thus do they behave. (27: 34)

The troops were given complete freedom to plunder the city for three days, and they made use of the opportunity with such enthusiasm that an English officer, Lord Lawrence, felt compelled to write to General Penny, the General-in-Command, in these strong words about the whole affair: "I believe we shall lastingly and, indeed, justly be abused for the way in which we have despoiled all classes without distinction."[100]

For three days, death and destruction reigned down up Delhi. People were slain indiscriminately, shops were looted, and houses were burnt. Men, women and children fled the town in their thousands. In the end, the city, which the day before had been the seat of Muslim splendour, was left in utter disarray. A graphic account of the ruin is found in the memoirs of Lord Roberts, who had led the English army from Kanpur to Delhi. This particular entry bears the date September 24th 1857, meaning it was made soon after the Red Fort of Delhi had fallen to the British. Lord Roberts writes:

> "That march through Delhi in the early morning light was a gruesome proceeding. Our way by the Lahore Gate from the Chandni Chowk led through a veritable city of the dead; not a sound was to be heard but the falling of our own footsteps; not a living creature was to be seen. Dead bodies were strewn about in all directions, in every attitude that the death struggle had caused them to assume, and in every stage of decomposition. We marched in silence or involuntarily spoke in whispers, as though fearing to disturb those ghastly remains of humanity. The sights we encountered were horrible and sickening to the last degree. Here a dog gnawed at an uncovered limb, there a vulture disturbed by our approach from its loathsome meal, but too completely gorged to fly, fluttered away

to a safer distance. In many instances the positions of the dead bodies were appallingly life-like. Some with their arms uplifted as if beckoning and, indeed, the scene was weird and terrible beyond description. Our horses seemed to feel the horror of it as much as we did, for they shook and snorted in evident terror. The atmosphere was unimaginably disgusting, laden as it was with the most noxious and sickening odours."[101]

An Islamic Rebellion

This was undoubtedly a general massacre, but the wrath seemed to be directed particularly against the Muslims, because many of the senior British figures associated the uprising with an Islamic jihad and believed that Muslims were the motivation behind it. To quote Henry Mead:

> "This rebellion, in its present phase, cannot be called a sepoy mutiny. It did begin with the sepoys, but soon its true nature was revealed. It was an Islamic revolt."[102]

Another narrator of this dreadful drama states:

> "An English officer had made it a principle to treat every Muslim as a rebel. He would enquire from everyone he saw if he was a Hindu or a Muslim and would shoot him dead right there if he turned out to be a Muslim."[103]

The Mass Execution of Muslims

After Delhi had been subdued and British control was firmly established, the public executions began. Scaffolds were erected on the thoroughfares and these places were considered centres of entertainment by the Englishmen. They would gather there in groups to enjoy the executions. Several localities of Muslims were totally wiped out.

> "Twenty-seven thousand Muslims were executed, to speak nothing of those killed in the general massacre. It seemed that the British were determined to blot out of existence the entire Muslim race. They killed the children and the way they treated the women simply belies description. It rends the heart to think of it."[104]

Lord Roberts writing to his mother on 21st June 1857 remarked: "The death that seems to have the greatest effect is being blown from a gun. It is rather a horrible sight, but, in these times, we cannot be particular." The purpose of this "business" was to show "these rascally Musalmans that, with God's help, Englishmen will still be the masters of India."[105]

The Price of the Struggle for Freedom

The Muslims, thus, had to pay most heavily for waging the struggle for freedom. The British held them to be the major offenders and decided that their future generations should also be made to bear the burden of their guilt. The attitude of the British bureaucracy can be gauged from the following quotation from Henry Harrington Thomas of the Bengal Civil Service in his pamphlet *Late Rebellion in India and Our Future Policy*, written in 1858 (just a year after the rebellion):

> "I have stated that the Hindus were not the contrivers or the primary movers of the 1857 rebellion and I now shall attempt to show that it was the result of a Mohammedan conspiracy... left to their resources, the Hindus never would or could have compassed

such an undertaking... They (the Mohammedans) have been uniformly the same from the times of the first Caliphs to the present day, proud, intolerant, and cruel, ever aiming at Mohammedan supremacy by whatever means, and ever fostering a deep hatred of Christians. They cannot be good subjects of any government which professes another religion; the precepts of the Quran will not suffer it."[106]

The Exclusion of Muslims from Public Services

This attitude towards Muslims continued to be the cornerstone of British policy in India for a long time. Muslims were barred from lucrative government jobs and were ejected from all other gainful occupations, their trade was ruined and 'the endowments from which their schools used to be maintained were confiscated. A system of education which ran counter to their cultural and intellectual ideals and aspirations was introduced deliberately in the country.[107]

It was sometimes openly stated in official notifications for government vacancies that only Hindus would be considered. Sir William Hunter reproduced the following extract from a Calcutta Persian paper (Durbiu), dated 14th July 1869.

> "Recently, when several vacancies occurred in the office of the Sundarbans Commissioner, that official, in advertising them in the Government Gazette, stated that the appointments would be given to none but Hindus."[108]

Commenting on this situation, the author goes on to say:

> "The Muslims have now sunk so low that, even when qualified for Government employment, they are stu-

diously kept out of it by government notifications. Nobody takes any notice of their helpless condition, and the higher authorities do not deign even to acknowledge their existence."[109]

Unconcealed Vindictiveness
The British made no attempt to conceal their ill-will against Muslims. They caught hold of them at the slightest excuse and showed no mercy. They waged a fierce war against the small band of mujahids beleaguered in the tribal belt of the North-West. Whoever was suspected by them of being in league with the mujahids or with the party of Syed Ahmad Shaheed was arrested and legal proceedings were started against him. Innumerable religious leaders, merchants and noblemen were tried on these grounds at Patna, Thanesar and Lahore, and sentenced to heavy terms of imprisonment. Some of them were branded as Wahhabis[110] and punished on that account.

Symptomatic of the immense British hatred towards the Muslims was the judgment delivered by an English judge while condemning the three alleged Wahhabi leaders Maulana Yahya Ali, Muhammad Jafar Thanesari and Muhammad Shafi Lahori to death. In the course of his judgment, the learned Judge remarked:

> "You will be hanged till death, your properties will be confiscated and your corpses will not be handed over to your relatives. Instead, you will be buried contemptuously in the jail compound."[111]

After the sentence of death had been passed, parties of English men and women visited the jail to see condemned prisoners in their cells and take delight in their sighs and groans. But when they found that the prisoners, instead of being sad and dejected, were actually revelling in their state and looking forward expectantly to the martyrdom that had so fortunately become their lot, they felt cheated and urged the Government to change their sentences to life-imprisonment. Ultimately, it was announced by the Deputy Commissioner of Ambala to the unfortunate men that the Chief Court had altered the death penalty passed against them to transportation for life. He said:

> "You rejoice over the sentence of death and look upon it as martyrdom. The Government, therefore, have decided not to award you the punishment you like so much. The death-sentence passed against you has been changed to that of transportation for life."[112]

The three prisoners along with two others, Maulana Ahmadullah Azimabadi and Molvi Abdul Rahim Sadiqpuri were then deported to the Andamans in 1865 where Maulana Yahya Ali and Maulana Ahmadullah died. The entire property of the family of Sadiqpur in Patna was seized by the Government, their houses were demolished and official buildings were constructed on their sites. The tombs of their ancestors were demolished. All this was done to quench the mad thirst for vengeance.

Several other noted ulema were sent to the Andaman Islands to serve life-sentences in banishment. These included Maulana Fazl-i-Haq Khairabadi, Mufti Inayat Ahmad Kakorwi and Mufti Mazhar Karim Daryabadi. Of these, Maulana Fazl-i-Haq met his death in exile while the other two returned home on completing their sentences. This policy of unmitigated spite and revenge was responsible for the political and educational backwardness that gripped the Muslims during the earlier stages of British rule and from which they have not yet been able to recover.

The Formation of the Indian National Congress

The first session of the Indian National Congress was held in 1884, and was attended by a number of prominent Muslim representatives. The fourth session at Madras in 1887 was presided over by a Muslim, Badruddin Tayyabji, and Muslim delegates drawn from different walks of life participated in it in sufficient numbers. A donation of 5,000 rupees by Mr Humayun Jah was announced in that session to the Congress.

Sir Syed Ahmad Khan's Disagreement

Initially, Sir Syed Ahmad Khan was a supporter of a common political platform, but he later changed his mind. His contention was that the political and educational backwardness of Muslims demanded that they should dissociate themselves from the national movement and avoid incurring the displeasure of the British Government by joining hands with the extremists of Bengal and other Hindu agitators. He felt that a separate non-political organisation would serve the interests of Muslims better. The alternative course, of political collaboration with the Hindus in opposition to the British, was fraught with the danger of reviving old wounds and creating fresh difficulties for them.[113]

The Support of the Ulema for the Congress

Notwithstanding Sir Syed Ahmad Khan's opposition, a large number of independent Muslims, under the leadership of the ulema, gave full support and cooperation to the nationalist activities and the Congress. They did not consider politics to be a forbidden arena for Muslims. In 1888, a whole set of religious decrees was published by Maulana Muhammad Saheb of Ludhiana urging Muslims to ally themselves with the Congress. These decrees were signed not only by prominent religious leaders of India like Maulana Rashid Ahmad Gangohi and Maulana Lutfullah of Aligarh but of Medina and Baghdad as well.

The Balkan War and its Repercussions in India

A wave of hatred and anger against the European Powers – and particularly Britain, which was their main power at the time – arose amongst Muslims with the outbreak of the Balkan War in 1912. The Islamic political consciousness, which had been steadily gaining in strength, reached its climax and burst in the East like a boil that had been festering for a long time. It was during these days that Maulana Abul Kalam Azad started publishing his fiery weekly paper, *al-Hilal*. It immediately became popular among Muslims and acquired a readership running into hundreds of thousands. Its trenchant criticism of Britain and the West was eagerly followed throughout the country. In addition to this, Maulana Muhammad Ali's English weekly, *Comrade* (originally published in Calcutta and later from Delhi), and Maulana Zafar Ali Khan's *Zamindar* (Lahore) and a host of other Muslim newspapers and periodicals helped to engender a strong anti-British sentiment amongst the educated sections of the community. As a result, Maulana Muhammad Ali, Maulana Shaukat Ali, Maulana Abul Kalam Azad and Maulana Hazrat Mohani were all arrested and imprisoned.

Maulana Mahmud Hasan of Deoband

The Principal of the Muslim religious institution of Deoband, Maulana Mahmud Hasan (who later came to be known as Shaykh al-Hind) was a sworn enemy of British Imperialism. No greater antagonist of the British had been seen in India since the time of Tipu Sultan. A staunch ally of the Ottoman Empire, since it symbolised the power of Islam in the world and also held the Muslim Caliphate, and an indefatigable fighter for India's freedom, he dedicated his whole life to the demise of the British Empire. He even established secret contacts with the Afghan Government and with the revolutionary leaders of Turkey like Enver Pasha.[114] He was taken into custody in 1916 by Sharif Husain at Medina in Arabia who handed him over to the British. The Maulana and his associates, Maulana Husain Ahmad Madani, Maulana Uzair Gut, Hakim Nusrat Husain and Molvi Waheed Ahmad, were deported to the Mediterranean island of Malta in 1917 where they remained until 1920.

Maulana Abdul Bari of Firangi Mahal

Maulana Abdul Bari of Firangi Mahal was another tireless champion of India's freedom. He organised the Jamiat Ulema-i-Hind to unite the Muslim religious leaders in the struggle for national independence and played a leading part in the Khilafat agitation. During his lifetime, Firangi Mahal in Lucknow functioned as the key-centre of Muslim politics.

The Rowlatt Report

In 1918, the Rowlatt Report made Muslims the main target of its attack and laid the blame for anti-British activities largely at their door. This further brought matters to a head.

The Khilafat Agitation and Hindu-Muslim Unity

A year later, the Ali Brothers, Muhammad and Shaukat Ali, were released and a wonderful spectacle of Hindu-Muslim unity was thereafter seen throughout India. The two communities put aside their differences and, linking their destinies together, marched forward as a single body, to do or die for the attainment of national freedom and preservation of the Ottoman Empire. The country was engulfed in a rare, revolutionary feeling.

India witnessed an incredible political awakening and was ablaze from one end to the other with resentment against the British masters. It was then that Gandhi made his debut on the nation's political stage. He undertook a countrywide tour in the company of Maulana Muhammad Ali and Maulana Shaukat Ali, addressing enormous public gatherings and arousing the masses for the national struggle for independence. Such a tremendous popular upsurge had never before been seen in India.

The Non-Cooperation Movement

In 1920, Gandhi and Maulana Abul Kalam Azad presented before the people the two programs of: non-cooperation with the British Government at all levels, and a boycott of foreign goods. The proposals were readily accepted by the masses as the major weapons of their movement, and they proved to be so effective that the Government was compelled to take full note of them. The British were threatened in India with a complete breakdown of the administrative machinery and a general insurrection. The inherent weakness of foreign rule was thoroughly exposed.

British Atrocities on the Moplahs

During the struggle for freedom, the severest loss of life and property was suffered by the Moplah Muslims of Malabar. Provoked by unmitigated tyranny and coercion, the Moplahs rose in armed revolt against the British Government on 21st August 1921. The rebellion, which lasted for a little over six months, reached such massive proportions that the Government had to even call in a warship to deal with it and they spent 5.1 million rupees between August and December alone on suppressing it. Thousands of Moplahs were killed.

In one instance of the ghastly atrocities perpetrated by the British, Moplah prisoners were herded together like cattle in the compartments of a railway train which three doctors had unanimously declared unfit for human transport. As a result, a great many of them perished on the journey; the British paying no heed to their cries of anguish and requests for water. The detainees were kept under close guard and subjected to all kinds of humiliation. After the rebellion had been quelled, and for a long time afterwards, Moplahs were denied ordinary civil liberties. The Committee of Inquiry appointed in 1922 by the Special Commissioner of Malabar reported that "there are at least 35,000 Moplah women and children whose condition is extremely miserable and unless proper measures are taken for their relief, many of them are likely to die of disease and starvation."

The Last Resort
The British Government in their desperation resorted to the favourite strategy of imperialists everywhere: divide and conquer, sowing the seeds of communal discord in the land. The then Viceroy took a prominent Hindu leader into his confidence and impressed upon him the need to start a powerful missionary movement to bring those who had embraced Islam back into the fold of Hinduism. The Viceroy also advised him how essential it was to organise his community on a militant basis, given that the Khilafah agitation had shown the strength, religious fervour and organisational capacity of the Muslims – the Hindus having foolishly allowed the initiative to pass into the hands of Muslims by making common cause with them on the issue of Khilafat, which was wholly a Muslim affair.

The Shuddhi, Sangathan and Tabligh Movements
This was the starting point of Hindu revivalist activities which, under the twin names of Shuddhi and Sangathan, spread all over India. In response, the Muslims established the Tabligh movement. An unending series of religious polemics, debates and conferences ensued, culminating, not unexpectedly, in violent communal disturbances.

The country was caught in the grip of terrible Hindu-Muslim riots. The Congress bravely stuck to its task in the midst of this fearsome madness and continued to hold its annual sessions regularly. A special session to discuss this tragic turn of events was summoned in 1922 under the presidency of Maulana Abul Kalam

The Role of Muslims in The Struggle for Freedom

Azad, while the regular annual session in the same year was held at Cocanada and presided over by Maulana Muhammad Ali.

Countrywide Communal Conflagration
The communal frenzy remained unchecked, peaking in 1927, when as many as twenty-five riots were recorded within the space of a few months. The nationalist sections of both communities were profoundly distressed at this state of events, but there seemed nothing they could do to restore communal peace and harmony. The gulf between Hindus and Muslims grew wider and wider. Eventually, this malady even began to cast its sinister shadow on the minds of the leaders of the two communities, until separating between Hindus and Muslims became a reality from which there was no escape.

The Parting of Ways
Both Hindu and Muslim intellectuals began to sense that the patriotism of the leaders of the nationalist movement was dwindling and they were becoming more and more divided into separate communal camps. Given that their thoughts and ambitions were essentially communal, they could no longer be seen to be adhering to the ideals of Indian nationalism in the hour of trial and opportunity. The Muslims felt in their hearts that the Hindu leaders (whose guiding spirit was now Gandhi) had failed lamentably to take adequate steps to combat the communal menace. They had not displayed the open-mindedness, impartiality and determination that was expected of them. By virtue of belonging to the majority community they wielded greater power and influence in the country, and could have, therefore, succeeded in putting down the riots, had they shown greater courage and objectivity, and denounced any communalists openly and without fear.

This Muslim view may have been wrong or exaggerated, but it alienated from the Congress many of the Muslim leaders, who had been in the vanguard of the nationalist movement. The Muslims, in general, were persuaded to believe that in order to safeguard effectively their rights and interests they would do better to rely on their own strength.

The Separate Muslim Front and the Demand for Partition
As a result, Maulana Muhammad Ali resigned from the Congress along with his friends and associates and joined the Muslim political camp. With the passing of time, the separatist instincts among Muslims became stronger. Muhammad Ali Jinnah revived the Muslim League in 1937 and within a few years it rose to be the most powerful representative organisation of Indian Muslims. After the League had consolidated its position, it raised the demand for the creation of Pakistan. Thanks to the anomalies of Indian society, the bitter experience of communal discrimination in official circles, the political immaturity of the people and inter-communal fears and suspicions, the country was eventually partitioned in 1947.

Maulana Husain Ahmad and the Jamiat Ulema-i-Hind
Muslim religious leaders connected with the Jamiat Ulema-i-Hind remained loyal to the Congress until the end. They did not waver in the least from their traditional nationalist stance.[115] In their forefront was Maulana Husain Ahmad Madani who, by his uncompromising hostility towards the British, his extraordinary patriotic zeal and his sincerity of purpose, proved himself to be a worthy successor of his teacher and mentor, Maulana Mahmud Hasan Deobandi. These ulema readily bore the opposition and disfavour of their co-religionists, a large majority of whom had come to share the views of the Muslim League. Maulana Madani strove to the best of his ability, during these fateful years, to make the Muslims realise the folly of the Pakistan demand. He undertook extensive tours of the country, preaching the gospel of unity

from town to town and village to village. Morally and religiously, his conduct remained absolutely spotless and above suspicion throughout that period of trial and crisis, and both friend and foe are unanimous in their praise of his integrity and sincerity. Even after independence, when countless opportunities for personal gain were open to him, he sought no favours for himself; he even politely declined to accept the title of Padma Vibhushan, conferred upon him by the President of India in 1954, saying that it was against the traditions of his predecessors to receive honours from the Government. Tragically, the high hopes he had entertained for freedom remained largely unfulfilled, and he was left frustrated and heart-broken. During the struggle he remained firm like a rock, and even after independence had been won there was no change in his political views and convictions.

Another leader of the Jamiat Ulema-i-Hind whose services cannot be overlooked is its General Secretary, Maulana Hifzur Rahman. The courage, resoluteness and enthusiasm with which he strove for the freedom of India before 1947 and has since then been displaying in safeguarding the rights and interests of Muslims, cannot easily be matched by other contemporary Muslim leaders. His heroic services during the post-independence communal riots will always be remembered with gratitude and admiration. He has never hesitated to expose the bitter truth regarding these outbreaks, in Parliament and elsewhere. Nor has he hesitated to criticise the local administration where it has been found to have behaved unjustly towards Muslims during any communal disturbances.[116]

Maulana Azad

Maulana Abul Kalam Azad had the distinction of serving as the President of the Congress for the largest number of years and at the most critical junctures of this nation's history. Two important British official missions, the Cripps Mission and the Cabinet

Mission, visited India during his final term of office to negotiate with the Indian leaders. The Maulana, as the President of the Congress, took an active part in the negotiations. The delegates, including Sir Stafford Cripps, were deeply impressed by his keen political foresight and acumen. It was during the Maulana's Presidency of the Congress that India attained freedom. His memoirs,[117] published shortly after his death, show that he played the role of a luminous mind in the machinery of the Congress. He gained universal respect for his sagacity and political insight. His contribution to the cause of freedom has been as profound as that of anyone anywhere.

Chapter 9
Current Difficulties and Problems

Trials and Hardships: A Necessity
At one stage or another, every nation or community will inevitably pass through a period of trial and hardship. These trials and hardships test its mettle and awaken within it the all-important will to live. They arouse and strengthen its latent potential; they turn the flint into fire. Nations that, from time to time, are not rocked by a calamity or brought face to face with a severe crisis lose the impulse for self-improvement; their self-confidence is shaken, and they eventually slip into sloth and complacency.

At present the Indian Muslims are passing through what may justly be described as highly testing times. They are confronted with a score of difficulties and problems. Some are of their own making, some a heritage from the past and some a product of the unsparing march of history. However, whatever they may be, they are, by the very nature of things, transitory. They are bound to disappear over the course of time, as long as Muslims grapple with them in a calm and disciplined manner, something possible only under a leadership that, in addition to being imaginative, courageous and honest, is also mature, balanced and realistic.

Here we will deal with some of these problems and hardships. We will leave aside the communal riots and disturbances for, although they constitute the biggest tragedy of free India today, they are, in our opinion, nothing more than a passing phenomenon in the evolution of our national life. Before long, the governmental machinery and the enlightened civic consciousness of our people will not fail to gain control over it. What are really alarming and deserve urgent and earnest attention are those questions that, like a slow fire, are sure to gradually destroy the very fabric of India's Muslims as a distinct religio-cultural entity.

Hindrances to Religious Preaching and Propagation
Firstly, there are the obstacles Muslims are experiencing in the field of religious preaching and propagation. Islam is a missionary religion. Throughout the world it has spread by preaching and proselytisation. In India, the number of Muslims who we have converted to Islam through the missionary efforts of its noble servants is much larger than those who have emigrated from other Islamic countries, such as Arabia, Iran and Turkey. This silent, unselfish propagation of Islam has kept the faith supplied regularly with new blood and a new spirit. It is through this channel that the brotherhood of Islam has always received fresh and worthy members who have subsequently made their mark on the entire Islamic world. The ancestry of many a distinguished Indian Muslim can be traced back to Hindus.

Among such men from the immediate past we can mention the names of Maulana Obaidullah Patialawi (the author of *Tuhfat al-Hind*), Maulana Obaidullah Sindhi, Dr Sir Muhammad Iqbal, Maulana Sanaullah Amritsari and Shaykh al-Tafsir Maulana Ahmad Ali Lahori. Few Muslims will know today that these distinguished brothers of theirs originally sprang from Hindu stock.

The missionary character of Islam was maintained even

through the declining days of Muslim power in India, right up to the termination of British rule. Every year, a considerable number of men would enter the Islamic fold of their own accord and free will and for the simple reason that Islam enjoyed superiority over other faiths because of its rationalistic teachings, solidly monotheistic creed and its enlightened concepts of universal brotherhood and social justice. There was no room in its social order for things like castes and untouchability. The glorious message of the Quran, the glittering example of the Prophet and the simple, impeccable precepts of the faith never ceased to conquer new minds and captivate new hearts. Had circumstances not changed, it is quite possible that Islam would have eventually emerged as the strongest religious force not only in the Subcontinent but the whole of Asia. Unfortunately, a grim political tussle ensued between Hindus and Muslims that rapidly assumed such awful proportions that it filled the two communities with anger and hatred of each other, and finally resulted in the division of the country into the two independent states of India and Pakistan. Whether this extreme step was proper or not and whether it was inevitable or could have been avoided is not for us to decide. We will leave the verdict to the historian of the future and confine ourselves to an examination of the atmosphere of mistrust and hostility that has become still heavier between these two communities in India as a consequence of Partition. One community looks upon everything characteristically associated with the other with suspicion and dislike, whether it relates to belief, thought or culture. This feeling of distrust and intolerance is proving to be the greatest barrier in the way of Islamic preaching and propagation. A general impression has been created in India about Islam that it is the religion of a state that was an unmistakable rival or enemy, and of a community with which bitter conflicts have taken place in the past. Memories of these conflicts are still fresh in the mind. To make matters worse, incidents also take place in Pakistan which have the effect of putting the clock back.

This, in short, is what is vexing Indian Muslims more than anything else today. However, we can confidently say that as time passes and relations between India and Pakistan improve, and as sanity begins to return to the Hindu-Muslim relationship in India, this gloomy state of affairs will disappear and Islam will regain its popularity and appeal. This is as long, of course, as Muslims pursue their missionary activities with wisdom and selfless devotion and without being in the least enamoured of considerations of political advantage and power. The very nature of the work demands that Muslims in this sphere be inspired solely by the ideal of service to mankind through enabling it to work out its salvation both in this world and the next. As a first step, they must set a high religious and moral example to their fellow countrymen. It will also be necessary, in the current context, to produce forceful Islamic literature of real merit and relevance to modern times in Hindi and other regional languages. Muslims must also participate wholeheartedly in the sphere of national development and reconstruction and discharge other patriotic duties with a full sense of responsibility and enthusiasm.

An Unjust and Partial System of Education
The next obstacle is that of education. This is of no less consequence to Muslims than the one we have just discussed. While difficulties in the path of their missionary endeavours hinder the progress of Islam, the current educational system strikes at the very roots of their existence as a separate religious and cultural community and throws their whole future in the country into jeopardy.

The Indian Constitution has guaranteed the freedom of creed and cultural development to all individuals and communities and bestowed a status of complete equality on all citizens irrespective of their religious affiliations. This Constitution is ideally suited to the conditions of our country, which has a heterogeneous population, with a number of religious and linguistic groups living side by side. In the same way, the needs of society will only be properly fulfilled by a system of education that fairly and faithfully represents the teachings of all the popular faiths in the land. Perhaps an arrangement like this is not possible in India in view of the great diversity of its religions. The next best alternative is to keep education strictly secular, in both design and content, as was the intention of those who framed the Constitution and as was the practice under the British regime. Such a course would give no cause for grievance to any religio-cultural community, including Muslims. Sadly, in the field of education, the secular ideal of the Constitution has remained only on paper. In most of the States, and in Uttar Pradesh in particular, courses of studies were introduced that were literally loaded with the religious beliefs and mythology of the majority community. A curriculum of this kind, naturally, militates against the very foundations of the Islamic faith, against its concepts of divinity and monotheism and against the Divine institution of prophethood.

A glance through the officially prescribed school textbooks unmistakably conveys the impression that those responsible for them regard the multi-religious country of India to be exclusively the home of Brahmins and attach value only to their deities, festivals, temples, pilgrim centres and religious customs and practices. The books recommended for general study, whose aim is to acquaint the children with their ancient heritage and the heroes of their history, deal solely with the ancient heritage and heroes of one community and ignore everything that is Muslim. One is struck with wonder at their inability to find in history a single Muslim spiritual leader, ruler or man of learning, who could be worthy of mention, given that there was no sphere of existence in which Islam did not produce personalities of the highest calibre, a study of whose lives could be tremendously inspirational for students. The heroes of the Muslim phase of Indian history have been treated by these writers as aliens and strangers, and if ever an Islamic personality has received their notice, it has been presented in the most unflattering, and even positively repulsive colours.[118] Even the Prophet himself has been mentioned in some books in terms completely at variance with the established facts of history. These books are based on an enormous amount of ignorance and prejudice and are a source of great pain for the 60 million Muslim citizens of India. At times, Muslims have even been described in these books as *yuwans*, meaning 'unclean' or 'foreigners'.

To include books of this type in school curricula and make their teaching compulsory for all children, including Muslims, is patently unjust to Muslims and a flagrant violation of their rights. It poses a serious threat to religious and cultural solidarity and to the religious survival of their future generations.

The Muslim fear that the new educational system is driving their children towards religious and intellectual apostasy is not imaginary. The destructive effects of the system can easily be seen in Muslim families that, for one reason or another, have been unable to maintain the basic ideals of Islamic Civilisation. The children of these families are progressively adopting un-Islamic and even manifestly polytheistic teachings and practices. This is, obviously, a highly distressing situation for Muslims.

Yet, we hope such a reactionary education system will not be allowed to continue for long. It is a passing phase, and the inherent democratic spirit of India, for which it is internationally famous, will not tolerate such an injustice to an important section of its population for long. The Government and India's educationists will step forward to put an end to this outrage against the Indian Constitution, whose consequences could be extremely harmful to the broader interests of the country.

At the same time, the current situation is exceedingly alarming for India's Muslims. A meeting of the Muslim Educational Conference was held at Basti in Uttar Pradesh towards the end of 1959 to vent their grievances in this regard. It was attended by over 300 delegates, representing all shades of Muslim opinion. The Conference called upon the Government to make necessary changes to the school syllabi by expunging from textbooks chapters that were hostile to the fundamental doctrines of the Islamic faith, or which were intended to propagate the religion and culture of one particular community, and thus restore to the educational system its secular character. The Conference also agreed to open private morning and evening classes for the theological instruction of school-going children and also to set up *maktabs* where the Quran, Islamic theology and Urdu could be taught alongside the subjects prescribed by the Government. The Conference obtained a heartening response from the Muslim community and now its branches are functioning in most of the towns of Uttar Pradesh.

The Question of Urdu
Then there is the question of language. The Urdu language is a product of the inter-mixing of various races, cultures and classes. It has its roots in as many as four classical languages: Sanskrit, Arabic, Persian and Turkish. Under the British regime, a large number of English words also made their way into the language. Urdu is therefore truly symbolic of the Indian national design. It started as a language of the masses and was later elevated to a language of cultural and literary expression through the joint efforts of intellectuals, poets and writers from different communities. With time, it came to meet the needs of modern journalism and express the aspirations of the national struggle. It blossomed into the most popular language of the country and became the greatest medium of communication and understanding among its various parts and communities. It is now the mother-tongue of the inhabitants of Uttar Pradesh, Punjab, Bihar, Hyderabad, Delhi and their surround-

ing areas. After some of the more important English newspapers, it is the journals appearing in Urdu, the dailies, weeklies and monthlies, that enjoy the largest circulation in India.

Under the British, Urdu was the second official language of the country, coming only after English. It was widely in use in schools, law-courts and government offices. Hindi was introduced into the field as a competitor for the first time in 1900 when Sir Anthony MacDonald, the then Lieutenant Governor of Uttar Pradesh, conferred recognition on it as a court language. In this way, discord was initially sown between the two languages, and, thoroby, between the people who spoke them.

Following Partition, the Constitution of the Indian Union decided in favour of Hindi as the official language, stating that: "The official language of the Union shall be Hindi in Devanagri script."[119] Apart from Hindi, fourteen other languages were also recognised as national languages, one or more of which could be adopted by the legislature of a State "as the language or the languages to be used for all or any of the official purposes of that State".[120] The President was further empowered to direct a State to recognise officially a language spoken by a substantial section of its population as its regional language, provided that he was satisfied that it was the mother tongue of a fairly large number of its inhabitants. Article 347 of the Constitution reads:

> "On a demand being made in that behalf the President may, if he is satisfied that a substantial proportion of the population of a State desire the use of any language spoken by them to be recognised by that State, direct that such language shall also be officially recognised throughout that State or any part thereof for such purpose as he may specify."

In spite of these safeguards, Urdu was dispensed with,

even from Delhi and Uttar Pradesh, where it had been born, flourished and attained maturity and which were its strongholds and natural home. It was expelled from schools as a medium of instruction at all stages, including the primary stage. In Uttar Pradesh, the Government undertook the task so thoroughly that Urdu was totally banned in practically all schools, government offices and law-courts.

This sudden turn of events took the Urdu-speaking sections of the community by surprise, and they were intensely perturbed and agitated over the treatment meted out to their mother tongue. This was particularly the case for the Muslims, since, in addition to their cultural and social loss, the banishment of Urdu had raised for them the question of the survival of their very creed and religion. Urdu was their sole instrument of contact with Islamic culture and civilisation. Their entire religious literature was in that language and its script was closely related to the Arabic script; knowledge of Urdu considerably facilitated reading the Quran. To deprive the Muslims of the Urdu language was like depriving them of their social and cultural identity and their spiritual inheritance. Consequently, the Urdu-speaking population vigorously protested against the official policy towards their language. The result was that a conference of provincial education ministers was held in Delhi during August 1949, and the following resolution was adopted regarding the medium of instruction in schools:

> "The medium of instruction and examination in the Junior Basic stage must be the mother-tongue of the child and where the mother-tongue is different from the Regional or the State language, arrangements must be made for instruction in the mother tongue by appointing at least one teacher, provided there are not less' than 40 pupils speaking the language in the

whole school or 10 such pupils in a class. The mother tongue will be the language declared by the parent or the guardian to be the mother tongue."

Unfortunately, the resolution turned out to be nothing more than a pious declaration. Hindi continued to be taught in the government and municipal schools of Uttar Pradesh not only as a compulsory subject but as the sole medium of instruction both at the basic and the secondary stages, and the teaching of Urdu was stopped altogether. Children whose mother tongue was Urdu were totally denied the opportunity to learn it, even in the junior, basic classes. Muslims and other Urdu-speaking people made repeated appeals to the Government to act on the resolution passed in Delhi during August 1949 and provide facilities for the teaching of Urdu to their children in schools. In the city of Lucknow alone, 10,000 parents and guardians petitioned the State Education Minister, but nothing changed. The minister promised to look into the matter, and then he apparently forgot about it.

When these efforts proved fruitless, the Urdu-speaking population decided to submit a memorial to the President of the Republic under Article 347 of the Constitution. A vigorous campaign was launched in the State of Uttar Pradesh for this purpose, under the direction of Anjuman Taraqqi-i-Urdu, and the signatures of no less than 2,050,000 adults and 2,000,000 children[121] were obtained for the memorial in a voluntary and peaceful manner. A deputation consisting of eminent public men and educationists, both Hindu and Muslim, was formed, with Dr Zakir Husain, the then Vice-Chancellor of Muslim University Aligarh and President of Anjuman Taraqqi-i-Urdu as its leader. It waited on the President on 15th February 1954 to present the memorial demanding the recognition of Urdu as the regional language of Uttar Pradesh. Other points made in the memorial were that facilities should be provided for children whose mother tongue was Urdu to receive instruction in that language at the primary stage; Urdu teachers should be appointed where there were at least ten pupils with Urdu as their mother tongue in a class or forty in a school; petitions and applications etc. written in the Urdu script should be entertained in government offices and law courts and given full consideration; all government notifications, bills, handouts and other publications should also be published in Urdu; awards should be granted by the Government to Urdu writers producing works of outstanding merit, as was formerly practiced, and their books should be bought by government libraries, academies and reading rooms to give them adequate encouragement; and, lastly, Urdu should again be given the status of a court language.

The deputation was received cordially by the President who gave it a patient hearing and showed sympathy with its demands, but that was the end of it. No action was taken on the memorial; the position of Urdu did not improve. It continued to be treated in a hostile manner by the authorities, and Urdu speaking children remained deprived, as before, of the right to receive instruction in their mother tongue. As a result, the link with their cultural past and the creed of their ancestors became weaker. The stage has now been reached where the rising generation of Muslims, for reasons already detailed, is finding itself separated, as if by centuries, from its spiritual and cultural roots. It is proving exceedingly difficult to re-establish this connection, since the bridge between the past and the present, that Urdu represented, has been destroyed.

More recently, in August 1961, a conference of Chief Ministers from different states was called by the Union Government in Delhi. There, what is commonly known as the Three Language Formula was evolved. According to this formula, students at the secondary stages will be required to study three languages: Hindi, English and some other Indian language. It was hoped that, in this way, Urdu speaking students would get the opportunity to study their mother-tongue in secondary schools. However, the Government of Uttar Pradesh thought otherwise and utterly disregarded the claim that Urdu was an Indian language, and so decided that the Formula did not apply to it. It held that the third language was to be one of the South Indian languages. This curious interpretation is another gross injustice to the unfortunate language. With the three compulsory languages and other subjects to be studied, the prospects of offering Urdu have become very slim. In practice, the result will be the ejection of Urdu from the secondary stage of education as well.

Also in 1961, a committee was set up by the Uttar Pradesh Government under the chairmanship of Acharya J. B. Kripalani to investigate the popular grievance that the government orders and directives with regard to the protection of Urdu were not being implemented and suggest suitable remedies. The report submitted by the committee has proved to be thoroughly disappointing. Instead of containing a single suggestion for meeting the grievances of the Urdu-speaking population, it has concerned itself mainly with Muslim *maktabs*, Islamic schools and Arabic and Persian madrasahs. If the recommendations of the Committee are accepted, the position of Urdu will be weakened further, and it will gradually lose its separate existence. The Muslim theological institutions which have been functioning in the State for over a century will also come to an end if the recommendations of the *Kripalani* Committee, which have been made with the avowed object of their betterment and reform, are acted upon.

The denial of justice to Urdu has thrown the Indian Muslims into a quandary and put them under tremendous strain. They are in danger of losing their personality in their own homeland. Despite this, we truly feel that the Muslims should not despair. As political awareness gathers greater force in India, a fair and just solution to the problem is bound to appear. Enlightened public opinion will ultimately realise the wisdom of satisfying the linguistic and cultural aspirations of Muslims and other Urdu-speaking sections of the population. It is not hard to see that an essential prerequisite of national progress and prosperity is that a climate of hope and confidence, in respect of their language, religion and culture, is created for the different communities that inhabit the country. The minorities must be made to feel that the days of arbitrary discrimination and exploitation are gone now that freedom has been won, and that no language, not even Hindi, will anymore be allowed to stand in the way of the development of the other languages. The Indian National Congress had unequivocally guaranteed the protection of the social, religious and cultural rights and interests of all communities and groups when it raised the banner of revolt against the British. The Indian people had marched united in the fight for freedom in the hope that, after the battle was won, the right of religious and cultural self-expression that had been snatched away from them by the alien rulers would be restored, and they would be free to develop and flourish according to their own needs and genius.

The Economic Problem

Lastly, there is the economic problem. There is no need to emphasise how important economic stability and security is to the mental and physical wellbeing of a people. There is nothing more degrading than constant financial distress and anxiety, for individuals as well as for communities. It destroys all that is good and noble in them, distorts their values, breeds frustration and a perpetual feeling of injustice, and eventually subjugates them to the level of a backward and depressed people. Their intellectual and spiritual springs soon dry up, and they become bereft of all creative impulses and the joy of living.

Until 1947, the main sources of income among Muslims were being a *zamindar* (landowner), government services and the higher branches of trade. After Independence, the *zamindari* landownership system was abolished, and to a great extent rightly too. As far as public services are concerned, the proportion of Muslims in them has been falling day by day. These two factors have brought the community to the verge of economic ruin. A community wide analysis of recruitment by various government departments during these years – particularly by the Armed Forces, the Police and other key services – will cause anyone unacquainted with the reality to conclude that either Muslims have completely migrated from India or they are altogether illiterate and unfit for government employment. This also helps to explain the fear Muslims have that, when the senior Muslim officers eventually retire from service, their representation in the bureaucratic and administrative set-up will virtually come to an end. No Muslim officer will be seen in government offices after that. The following authoritative comments and statistics support this contention. Firstly, there is this extract from Pandit Nehru's address to the All-India Congress Committee in Delhi on 11th May 1958:

> "I called for statistics from the states to ascertain the percentage of minorities in the recruitments to public services. I found that the representation of Muslims was progressively declining; one of the reasons being the procedure adopted for competitive examinations that are held for recruitment to All-India services. In these examinations, insistence is laid on the knowledge of Hindi and candidates who fail to qualify in it are rejected. Question papers are also required to be answered in Hindi and candidates belonging to minority communities find it hard to come up to the standard of literary Hindi."

Furthermore, it was admitted officially in the Delhi State Legislature (in 1952) that:

"The number of Muslims in the Delhi Police Force in 1946, was 1470; now it has dwindled to 56. Since 1946, only two Muslim Constables and one Head Constable have been recruited. The total strength of the Force today is 2058."

In other words, between 1946 and 1952, only three Muslims were recruited by the Delhi Police Force.

The speech delivered by Mahavir Tyagi, the Union Minister of State for Defence, in the Muslim University Union, Aligarh, tells the same tale. The Minister of State observed:

"The percentage of Muslims in the Armed Forces which was 32 at the time of Partition has now come down to 2. To correct this state of affairs, I have instructed that due regard should be paid to their recruitment."

These extracts speak for themselves. They leave no one in doubt as to what the position of the Muslims is today in the higher services, though they still possess the same qualities of head and heart which, up until a short time ago, used to qualify them for the highest appointments. This is also despite the fact that the standard of education amongst Muslims has been steadily rising. The Constitution of India has guaranteed equality of opportunity to all citizens whatever their caste or creed. One of the results of the policy of unconcealed discrimination is that, frustrated in their attempts to find suitable employment in the land of their birth, many educated Muslim young men are migrating every year to Pakistan.

In conclusion, these are some of the major problems and hardships that are bedevilling Indian Muslims at the present juncture of their history. In some ways, such a situation is not unexpected in a country which has just emerged from a long spell of foreign rule, and it is in this that hope for the future lies. Logically, this phase can only be temporary; it cannot go on forever. The clouds will disperse and there will be sunshine again. The Muslims will regain their position in the country that is justly theirs. All the schemes for national reconstruction will remain incomplete if they are left to rot and decay. But, for that, Muslims will have to produce within themselves an undying faith in God. They will have to cultivate the virtues of patience and steadfastness of purpose and convincingly prove their worth, merit and usefulness to this nation.

Appendix

The population of Indian Muslims, according to the Census of India, 1971, is 61,417,934 or 11.21 percent of the total population of India. The breakdown of the population figures of Indian Muslims between males and females is 31,961,789 and 29,456,145 respectively, while the ratio of urban to rural population is 16.21 to 9.97 per cent. In terms of percentages, the population of Indian Muslims has increased from 10.7 in 1961 to 11.21 in 1971, showing an increase of 0.51 points. During the previous decade 1951-61 the increase was from 9.91 to 10.7 percent, i.e. 0.79 points.

Given below are three tables showing the distribution of the Muslim population of India according to State, the distribution of the Muslim population according to District, and the percentage increase/decrease of Muslims according to State during the decade 1961-71.

Table I: The distribution of the Muslim population of India according to State, as recorded in the 1971 Census.

State	Total Population	Muslims	Muslims as a Percentage of the Total Population
INDIA	547,949,809	61,417,934	11.21
Andhra Pradesh	43,502,708	3,520,166	8.09
Assam	14,957,542	3,594,006	24.03
Bihar	56,353,369	7,594,173	13.48
(Gujarat)	26,697,475	2,249,055	8.42
Haryana	10,036,808	405,723	4.04
Himachal Pradesh	3,460,434	50,327	1.45
Jammu and Kashmir	4,616,632	3,040,189	65.85
Kerala	21,347,375	4,162,718	19.5
Madhya Pradesh	41,654,119	1,815,685	4.36

Appendix

Maharashtra	50,412,235	4,233,023	8.4
Manipur	1,072,753	70,969	6.61
Meghalaya	1,011,699	26,347	2.6
Mysore	29,299,014	3,113,298	10.63
Nagaland	516,449	2,966	0.58
Orissa	21,944,615	326,507	1.49
Punjab	13,551,060	114,447	0.84
Rajasthan	25,765,806	1,778,275	6.9
Tamil Nadu	41,199,168	2,103,899	5.11
Tripura	1,556,342	103,962	6.68
Punjab	13,551,060	114,447	0.84
Uttar Pradesh	88,141,144	13,676,533	15.51
West Bengal	44,312,011	9,064,338	20.46

Union Territories			
Andaman and Nicobar Islands	115,133	11,655	10.12
Arunachal Pradesh	476,511	842	0.18
Chandigarh	257,251	3,720	1.45
Dadar and Nagar Haveli	74,140	740	1
Delhi	4,065,698	263,019	6.47
Goa, Daman and Diu	857,771	32,250	3.76
Pondicherry	471,707	29,141	6.18

Table II: Distribution of the Muslim population according to District.

Category	No. of Districts
Up to l 2.5 per cent	81
From 2.51 to 5.00	51
From 5.01 to 10.00	102

Appendix

From 10.01 to 20.00	83
From 20.01 to 50.00	30
From 50.01 and above	9

Table III: Percentage increase and decrease of Muslims according to State during the decade 1961-71

State	Percentage of the Total Population		% Increase (+) or Decrease (-)	
	1961	1971		
Kerala	17.91	19.5	+	1.59
Goa, Daman & Diu	2.33	3.76	+	1.43
Bihar	12.45	13.48	+	1.03
Uttar Pradesh	14.63	15.48	+	0.85
Mysore	9.87	10.63	+	0.76
Maharashtra	7.67	8.4	+	0.73
Delhi	5.85	6.47	+	0.62
Andhra	7.55	8.09	+	0.54

Tripura	20.14	6.68	13.46
Laccadive, Minicoy and Aminidivi Islands	98.68	94.37	4.31
Jammu and Kashmir	68.3	65.85	2.45
Assam	24.7	24.03	0.67
Meghalaya	2.99	2.6	0.39
Pondicherry	6.36	6.18	0.18
Gujarat	8.46	8.42	0.04
Andaman and Nicobar Islands	11.64	10.12	1.52

Source: Census of India, Series, Paper 2 of 1972.

Index

PERSONALITIES
Abdul Ali, Maulana, BahrulUloom 95, 96
Abdul Ali, Dr. Syed 108
Abdul Aziz, AbulQasim 57
Abdul Aziz, Shah, Dehlavi 45
Abdul Aziz Memon, Maulana 47
Abdul Bari, Firangi Mahal 130
Abdul Bari, Maulana, Nadwi 167
Abdul Hayy, Maulana Burhanawi 99
Abdul Hayy, Maulana, FirangiMahal 41, 94
Abdul Hayy, Maulana, El-Hasani 163
Abdul Hakim, Dr., Khalifa 167
Abdul Hakim, Mulla, Sialkoti 94, 96
Abdul Huq Muhaddith Dehlavi 43
Abdul Huqq Dr., Molvi 117
Abdul Huqq Haqqani 108
Abdullah Khan, Nawab 75
Abdullah Yusuf Ali 46
Abdul Latif, MaulanaSaharanpuri 105
Abdul Latif, Dr., Syed 167
Abdullah, Maulana, al-Emadi 117
Abdullah, Maulana, Badayuni 94
Abdul Majid, Maulana, Daryabadi 45, 46, 117
Abdul Muqtadir, Kindi 47, 74, 98
Abdul Nafey, Molvi 95
Abdul Qadir, Mulla, Badayuni 94
Abdul Qaiyum, Mulla 115
Abdul Rahman, Maulana, Mubarakpuri 44
Abdul Rahman, Maulana, Kamilpuri 105
Abdul Rahim, Khan-i-Khanan 47, 57
Abdul Rahim Maulana, Rampur 93
Abdul Rahim, Maulana, Sadiqpuri 127
Abdul Razzaq Bansawi 99, 100
Abdul Razzaq, Khawafi 58
Abdul Razzaq, Molvi, Malihabadi 48
Abdul Salam, Maulana, Lahori 94
Abdul Shakoor Faruqi, Maulana 45

Abdun-Nabi Ahmednagri 39
Abu A'la Mawdudi, Munlana, Syed 46
Abul Fazl 58, 59
Abul Hasan, el-Bakri el Shafai, Sheikh 37
Abul Kalam Azad, Maulana 48, 129, 131, 132, 135
Adam, Syed, Bannuri 66
Ahmad Ali, Maulana, Lahori 108, 138
Ahmad Ali, Muhaddis, Saharanpuri 108
Ahmad Amethwi, Maulana (Mulla Jiwan) 94
Ahmad ibn Muhammad, Thanesari 47
Ahmad Saeed, Maulana 114
Ahmad Shaheed, Hazrat, Syed 61, 67, 68, 70, 71, 74, 99, 126
Ahmad Farooqi, Sirhindi, Sheikh, Mujaddid Alf-Sani 45, 60, 65
Ahmadullah, Maulana, Azimabadi 127
Ahmadullah, Maulvi 127
Ajmal Khan, Hakim 112
Aziz Ali, Maulana 104
Akbar, Emperor 28, 96
Alauddin, Khilji 52, 68, 75
Alauddin, Shaykh-ul-Islam 69
Alexander, the Great 21
Ali Asghar, Maulana, Kannauji 94
Ali Akbar Husayni, Sheikh 39
Ali Bin Shahab Hamadani, Kashmiri 19
Ali Hakim, Gilani 94
Ali Hasan, Khan, Nawab, Syed 108
Ali bin Husamuddin, Shaykh, el-Muttaqi Burhanputi Shaykh Ali Muttaqi Gujarati 37
Ali Hujweri, Syed, Hazrat 19
Ameer Ali, Syed 46
Amir Khusro 47
Anwar Shah, Maulana, Kashmiri 44, 104, 107, 165
Anwar Ullah, Khan (Maulana) 115
Asadullah, Maulana 105
Asaf Jah, Nawab 77
Asaf Khan 57
Asghar Husayn, Syed, Maulana 104
Ashraf Ali, Maulana, Thanwi 41, 105
Ataullah Shah Bukhari 169
Athar Ali, Munshi, Kakorwi 108
Awhaduddin Bilgrami 47
Aurangzeb, Emperor 38, 54, 61
Azimullah, Khan 167
Azizur Rahman (Mufti) 104
Babar, Emperor 27
Badrudin, Tayyabji 128
Bahadur Shah Zafar, Emperor 120
Bakht Khan, General 167
Baqar ibn Murtuza, Maulana, Madrasi 41
Beck 168
Bosworth Smith 168
Bernier, Francois 163
Carra de Vaux 59, 165
Chengiz Khan 52
Cripps, Sir Stafford 136
Dumyati, El 36
Edwaed Thompson 168
Ehtisham Ali, Munshi, Kakorwi 108
Faizul Hasan, Maulana, Saharanpuri 47
Fariduddin Ganj Shakar, Khwaja 70
FarrukhSiyar, Emperor 74, 75
Fathullah Shirazi 96
Fazl-i-Haq, Molvi, Khairabadi 127
Fazlur Rahman, HazratMaulana, Ganj Moradabad 78, 99, 101
Fyzee 58, 59
Gandhi 130, 131, 133, 167
Ghiyasuddin Balban 52
Ghulam, Naqshband, Maulana 99

Ghulam Ali Azad, Bilgrami 47, 95, 97
Ghulam Ali, Shah, Dehlavi 66, 67, 77
Ghulam Rasul, Maulana 104
Ghulam Rasool Mehr 165, 168
Gustave le Bon 24, 163
Habibur Rahman Khan Sherwani (Maulana) 108, 114, 118
Habibur Rahman Ludhianwi (Maulana) 169
Hajji Khalifa 35, 99
Hali, Altaf Husain, Khwaja 90
Hamid, Sheikh, Jaunpuri 39
Hamiduddin, Farahi, Maulana 44
Hamidullah, Dr. 167
Hariri 40
Harun Khan Sherwani 167
Hazrat Mohani, Maulana 129
Hasan ibn Muhammad al-Saghani Lahori 36
Hashim, Nadwi, Syed Maulana 167
Hawkins 93
Hazrat Mahal, Begum 167
Henry Mead 123
Hifzur Rahman, Maulana 135, 168
Harris, General 120
Holmes 167
Humayun Kabir 163
Humayun Jah, Mr 128
Hunter, w. w. 32, 164, 165, 168
Husain Ahmad Madani, Maulana 130, 134
Husain Syed Imad-ul-Mulk, Bilgrami 115
Ibrahim, Prophet 82, 87, 166
Ibrahim Abu Muhammad, Aarwi Maulana 108
Ibrahim Sharqi, Sultan 96
Ibrahim, Shaykh, al-Jibali 116
Ibn Battuta 88

Ibn Hajar, Shahabuddin, al-Makki 57
Ibn Jubayr 88
Ibn-Khaldun 40 60
Ilyas Bari 167
Imaduddin Gilani (Mahmud Gawan) 57
Imdadullah, Hazrat Hajji 66, 99, 100, 101
Inayat Ahmad, Mufti Kakorwi 127
Inayat Elahi, Maulana 105
Inayatullah, Molvi, Dehlavi 117
Ismail Shaheed, Maulana, Dehlavi 45, 60
Jamal Pasha 168
Jamshed 78
Jawaharlal Nehru, Pandit 22
Jahangir, Emperor 27
Jinnah, Muhammad Ali 134
Jiwan, Mulla 94
Kalb-i-Ali Khan, Nawab 78
Kamaluddin Hyder 168
Kamaluddin, Syed, Azimabadi 95
Kanakuddin, Khwaja 46
Karamat Hussain, Justice 45
Khaleel Ahmed Saharanpuri, Maulana 43, 105
Khalid Rumi, Maulana 66
Khalid Shahrazori Kurdi 61
Khalid Naqshbandi 165
Khlilur Rahman, Maulana, Saharanpuri 108
Khizr, Khan 75
Khwaja, Maulana Dehlavi 98
Kifayatullah, Maulana, Mufti 168
Kripalani, Acharya, J. B. 148
Lawrence, Lord 122
Liaquat Ali, Maulana 167
Lutfullah, Maulana (Aligarh) 128
MacDonald, Anthony 144

Mahmud Hasan, (Sheikhul-Hind) 112, 129, 134,
Mahmud, Mullah Jaunpuri 44, 95
Mahmud Gawan 57
Mahavir Tyagi 151
Mahbub Ali Khan, Mir 108
Mahmud Ghazni 19, 164
Mahmud Shah, Sultan (Mahmud Baigrah) 28
Mahmud Shah (II) Malwa 54
Majduddin al-Fayruzabadi, Allama 40
Manazir Ahsan Gilani, Maulana 45, 75, 166
Mandli Rai 54, 55,
Marshman Clarke 53, 165
Masihuzzaman, Maulana 108
Masood Alam, Nadwi, Maulana 48
Mazhar Karim, Daryabadi 127
Mazhar, Mirza, Jan-i-Janan 77
Mehta, N. S. 32
Mir Dard, Khwaja 73
Mir khan 77
Muhammad Abbas, Mufti, Lakhnavi 41, 47
Muhammad Abid, Hajji 104
Muhammad Abu Dhahab 41
Muhammad Afzal, Maulana 95
Muhammad Akram, Mufti, Lahori 39
Muhammad Aslam, Kazi, Harawi 96
Muhammad Ashraf, Maulana, Dayanawi 43, 164
Muhammad Askari Naqvi 48
Muhammad A'la, Thanwi 39
Muhammad Ali, Maulana, Mongyri 107
Muhammad Ali, Maulana 107, 112, 129, 130, 133, 134
Muhammad Amin Ibn 'Umar 'Abidin 165

Muhammad ibn Tughluq (Sultan) 72
Muhammad el-Hassani 18
Muhammad Ghori 19
Muhammad Ghaus, Sheikh, Gwaliori 99
Muhammad Husayn, Qadi, Jaunpuri 39
Muhammad Ilyas, Maulana 62, 105
Muhammad Imran, Khan, Nadwi 110
Muhammad Iqbal, Dr. Sir 138
Muhammad Jafar, Maulana, Thanesari 126, 168
Muhammad Jaisi, Malik 47
Muhammad Masoom, Khwaja 65, 67
Muhammad Mazhar, Maulana, Nanautawi 105
Muhammad Qasim, Maulana, Nanautawi 45, 99, 100, 104, 105
Muhammad Qasim, Bijapuri (Farishta) 96
Muhammad Saeed, Syed (Shah Bheek) 74
Muhammad Saheb, Maulana (of Ludhiana) 128
Muhammad Shafi Lahori 126
Muhammad Surti, Maulana 47
Muhammad Yahya, Maulana 105
Muhammad Yaqub, Maulana, Nanautawi 104
Muhammad Zakariyya, Maulana Kandhlawi 44
Muhammad Zahir, Maulana 47
Mohiuddin Qadri, (Zor) 167
Mohibullah, Allama, Bihari 39
Moinuddin, Khwaja, Ajmeri 19, 66
Morrison 168
Muhammad Hasan of Tonk 42
Mujaddid al-Alf al-Thani (Hazrat) 61

Mukhtar Ahmad Ansari, Dr. 112
Murtada, Syed, Bilgrami, Allama 40
Muzaffar Halim (Muzaffar Shah of Gujarat) 54
Nasiruddin, Chiragh Dehlwi, Sheikh Khwaja 74, 98
Nasir Hasan, Syed, Kintoori 74
Nazeer Husain, Syed, Maulana, Dehlavi 118
Nehru, Jawaharlal 22, 27, 30, 163
Nizamuddin Awliya, Hazrat, Khwaja (Sultan ul-Mashaikh) 70, 74, 79
Nizamuddin, Mulla (Firangi Mahal) 95, 99, 100, 167
Nizamuddin, Sheikh, Burhanpuri 38
Nizamuddin, Dr. 167
Nuruddin 72
Nusrat Husain, Hakim 130
Obaidullah, Patialawi (Maulana) 138
Obaidullah Sindhi (Maulana) 138
Osman Ali Khan, Nizam of Hyderabad Dn. 115
Panikkar k.M. 21, 163
Pir Muhammad, Shah 99
Penny, General 122
Plato 25
Qasim (Sheikh), Daryabad 47
Qazim Qalandar, Shah 47
Qutubuddin, Aibak 164
Qutbuddin Munawwar, Sheikh 71
Rafiuddin, Shah Dehlavi 60
Rahat Ali, Molvi 47
Rahim Bx, Sir 108
Rahmatullah, Maulana, Kairanwi 44
Rana Sanga 55
Rashid Ahmad, Maulana, Gangohi 99, 101, 105, 128
Rashid Rida, Syed 43
Raziuddin Siddiqui, Dr. 167

Riqullah, Maulana, Dehlavi 47
Roberts, Lord 122, 124, 168
Roshan-ud-Daula 74, 75
Ruknuddin, Shaikhul Islam 69
Sa'adat Ali, Saharanpuri, Maulana 105
Sabahuddin Abdul Rahman 114, 164
Sabit Ali (Maulana) 105
Sadar Yar Jung 114, 118
Sadruddin, Munshi 95
Sadruddin, Mufti, Dehlavi 47
Saeed Ahmad, Maulana, Akbarabadi 114
Saifuddin Sirhindi, Sheikh 74
Sajjad, Maulana, Bihari 114
Salim III, Sultan of Turkey 119
Sanaullah, Kazi, Panipali 44
Sanaullah, Maulana, Amritsari 108, 138
Shabbir Ahmad Osmani 44
Shah jahan, Emperor 28
Shahabuddin, Daulatabadi Qazi 96
Shahabuddin Ibn-i-Hajar El Makki 57
ShamshulHaqDayanayi, Manlana 164
Shah Alam, Emperor 73
Shamshuddin, Iltutmish 52
Sharafuddin Yahya Maneri, Sheikh 60
Sharif Husain 129
Shaukat Ali, Maulana 129, 130
Sher Shah 28, 29, 53
Shibli Nomani, Maulana 113
Siddiq Hasan Khan of Bhopal 41
Sitaramayya, Dr., Pattabhi 30
Sircar, Jadunath 31
Sulaiman Nadwi, Syed, Maulana 42, 45, 110, 113
Sulaiman Ashraf, Syed, Maulana 45
Sulaiman, Qadi, Mansurpuri 108
Sulaiman, Shah, Phulwarawi, Maulana 108
Syed Mubarak, Mir 92

Syed Ahmad Khan, Sir 67, 111, 114, 128
Syed Ali, Bilgrami 163
Syed Husain, Bilgrami 115
Suyuti, Allama 36, 37, 164
Tahir Pattani, Allama 37
Talammuz Husayn, Qadi 117
Timur 27
Tipu Sultan 119, 120, 129
Thomas, Henry Harrington 124
Tufail Ahmad Bilgrami, Mir 92
Usman al-Sanad 165
Uzair Gut 130
Vaux, Carra, de 59, 165
WalaJah, Nawab 95, 97
Wajihuddin, Allama, Gujarati 94, 98
Wahiduddin Saleem, Molvi, Panipati 117
Waheed Ahmad, Molvi 130
Waliullah Shah, Dehlavi 60
Waliullah, Molvi Firangi Mahli 96
Waliuddin, Dr., Mir 167
WaqarulMulk, Nawab 115
Yahya Ali, Maulana 126, 127
Yusuf (Joseph) 165
Zafar Ali Khan, Maulana 129
Zakaullah, Munshi 168
Zaheer Ahsan Shauq, Meemwi 44, 164
Zahid, Mir 96
Zahir Husain, Dr., 112
Zarif, syed, Azimabadi 95
Zarradi, Maulana Fakhruddin 72
Ziauddin, Barani 19, 52
Zulfiqar Ali Maulana, Deobandi 47

BOOKS AND MAGAZINES

Asar-us-Sanadeed 67
Aathar al-Sunan 44
Abjad al-'Ulum 41
Abu al-'Ala' wa ma ilayh 47

Aghsan-I-Arba'a 167
Ain-i-Akbar 29, 59
AkbarNama 59
Al-'Alam al-Khaffaq 41
Al-Ba'th al-Islami (Al-Ba'as-ul-Islami) 48
Al Muslimun 16
Al-Nabiy al-Khatim 42
Awjaz al-Masalik 44
Asfa al-Mawarid 165
Bang Darpan 47
Badhl al-Majhud 43
Burhan 114
Commentary of the Qur'an 45, 46, 110
Comrade 129
Discovery of India 163
Al-Bayan 41, 48
al-Bulghah Fi Usul al-lughah 41
Al-Fara'id 44
Al-Fawa'id al-Bahiyyah 41
Al-Hilal 129
Al-Imam fi Aqsam al-Qur'an 44
El-Mubin 45
El-Qamus Al-Muhit 40
El-Ridwan 48
Al-Taj al-Makallal 41
Al-'Ubab al-Zakhir 36
Al-Yaqazah 48
Al-Nabiy al-Khatim 42, 45
Al-Thaqafah al-Islamiyyah fi al-Hind 36, 24
Al-Ta'liq al-Mumajjad 41
Fayd al-Bari 44
Fatawa-e-Alamgiri 38
Fath al-Bayan 41
Fath al-Mulhim 44
Fawa'id al-Fuwad 165
Fiqh al-Lisan 45
GhayantulMaqsood 164

Gul-i-Ra'ana 166
HamarePurwaj 169
Hans Jawahar 47
Al-Hidayah 38
Hindustan ke Ahd-i-Wusta Ki Ek Jhalak 164
History of the Saracens 46
Hujjat al-Islam 45
Huijatullah al-Balighah 39, 40
Ideal Prophet 46
Indian Musalmans 164, 165, 168
India Wins Freedom 169
Islam in India 31, 58,
IzalatulAuham 44
Izalat al-shukuk 44
Izalat al-Khafa' 45
Izhar al-huq 44
Jami' al-Ulum 39
Jam' al-Jawami' 37
Jannat al-Mashriq 29
Jawharat al-Balaghah 44
Joot Nitranjan 47
Kanz al-'Ummal 36
Kashf-ul-Zunoom 35
Kashshaf Istilahat al-Funun 39
Khutbat-l-Madras 45
Lisan al-Arab 47
Ma'arif 42, 114
Ma'asir al-Kiram 166, 167
Ma'athir al-Umara' 58
MAjma' Bihar al-Anwar 37
Manaqib-i-Razzaqia 99
Mansab Imamah 45
Mashariq al-Anwar 36
Maulana Muhammad Ilyas 62, 105
Miftah Kunuz al-Sunnah 43
Mirat-i-Sikandari 165
Misbah al-Duja 41
Mu'ajam al-Musannifin 42

Muntakhab al-Tawarikh 166
Musallam al-Thubut fi Usul al-Fiqh 39
Nizame Taleem-o-Tarbiat 42, 166
Nuzhat al-Khawatir 37, 62, 163, 165, 166
Other side of the Medal (The) 168
Padmavat 47
Paimain 47
Penseur de Islam 165
Prem Prakash 47
Qaisar al-Tawarikh 166
Rahmatun lil-'Alamin 45
Ramayana 24, 25
Sahih al-Bukhari 44
Sall al-Husam al-Hindi 165
Sirat Syed Ahmad Shaheed 45, 61, 67, 68, 70, 71, 99, 126, 165
Sarv-i-Azad 47
Sirat al-Nabi 45
Sher al-Ajam 45
Siyar al-'Arifin 166
Siyar al-Awliya' 166
Simt al-La'ali 47
Al-Sirat al-Mustaqim 45
Sources of Christianity 46
Spirit of Islam 46, 60, 66
Sunan Abi Dawud 43, 164
Tadween-e-Hadith 42
Tafhimat 46
Tafsir Mazhari 44
Tafsir Ma'alim al-Tanzil 56
Taj al-'Arus min Jawahir al-Qamus 40
Tanqihat 46
Taqrir-i-Dipizir 45
Tarikh-i-Dawat-o-Azimat 165
Tarikh-i-Farishta 96
Tarikh-i-Gujarat 167
Tarjuma al-Qur'an 46
Tazkirah 46

Tazkira-i-Adamiya 67
Tazkira-i-Ulema-e-Hind 166
Tiqsar 165
Al-Tuhfa al-Isna al-'Ashariyyah 45
Tuhfa-i-Muhammadiyah 107
Tuhfat al-Hind 138
Tuhfat al-Ahwadhi 44
Tuzuk-i-Babari 26, 27
Tuzuk-i-Jahangiri 27
Uruj-i-Sultanat-i-Englishia 168
Zafar al-Amani 41

BODIES, INSTITUTIONS and MOVEMENTS
All India Congress Committee 150
All India Muslim League 134
Anjuman Taraqqi-i-Urdu 146
Arab League 118
Arabic Academy 163
Asafia Library 42
Dairatul Ma'arif 15, 116, 164
Darul Uloom Deoband 9, 48, 96, 99, 103
Darul Uloom Nadwatul Ulama 107
Darul Uloom Bhopal 110
Darul Musannifin 113
Darul Tarjuma 116, 117
Din-i-Ilahi 53
Dini Talimi Board 10, 115
Dini Talimi Council 10, 115
El-Baqiyat us-Salehat 107
Farooq College 113
Indian Council for Cultural Relations 13
Indian National Congress 128, 149
Jama'at-i-Islami 117
Jamal Muhammad College 113
Jamia-i-Ashrafia (Rander) 107
University of al-Azhar 41, 116

Jami'a Ahmadiyah 110
Jami'a Millia 112
Jami'a-i-Darus Salam 107
Jami'a-i-Husainia 107
Jami'a Osmania (Osmania University) 113
Jami'at-i-Ulema-i-Hind 115, 130, 134, 135
Khuda Bux Library 117
Kutub Khana-i-Asafia 118
Kutub Khana-i-Darul Uloom Deoband 118
Kutub Khana-i-Maulana Habibur Rahman Sherwani 118
Library of Nasir-ul-Millet 118
Madrasa-i-Ahmadiah Salafia 106
Madrasa-i-'Alia, Calcutta 106
Madrasa-i-'Alia, Rampur 106
Madrasatul Islah 9, 110
Madrasa-i-Imdadia of Darbhanga 106
Madrasa-i-Jamalia 107
Madrasa-i-Rahmania, Delhi 106
Madrasa-i-Rahmania, Varanasi 106
Madrasa-i-Shamshul Had 106
Madrassatul Uloom (M. A. O. College Aligarh) 111
Madrasa-i-Nizamiya 106, 107
Madrasatul Waizeen 106
Madinatul Uloom 107
Majlis-i-Tahqiat-o-Nashriyat-i-Islam 114
Mazahir Uloom, Saharanpur 105
Muslim Educational Conference 114
Muslim University, Aligarh 111, 146, 151
Nadwatul Musannifin 114
Nadwatul Ulama 48, 99, 108, 109, 110
New College 113
Non-co-operation Movement 131

Osmania College of Kurnool 113
Rauzatul Uloom 107
Raza Library (Rampur) 117, 118
Shahi Madrassa of Moradabad 106
Sir Salar Jung Museum 118
Sullam-us-Salam 107
Sultanul Madaris 106

PLACES
Ahmedabad 98, 164
Aligarh 110, 111, 128, 151
Allahabad 67, 97
Ambala 75, 127
Amethi 99
Anand 107
Azamgarh 110, 113, 118
Baghdad 52, 66, 128
Basti 143
Beirut 42
Bhopal 41, 110
Bihar 143, 164
Bilgram 47
Burdwan 95
Calcutta 48, 67, 70, 106, 118, 125, 129
Calicut 107, 113
Cocanada 133
Dabhel 107
Dacca 163
Damascus 16, 163
Darfoor 41
Delhi 41, 62, 70, 72, 74, 75, 77, 79, 88, 106, 110, 112, 114, 120, 121, 129, 143, 145, 150, 167
Deoband 48, 99, 101, 103, 104, 106, 129
Darbhanga 106
Gangoh 74, 101,
Ghazipur 67
Hyderabad 42, 88, 107, 108, 110, 113, 115, 116, 117, 118, 143, 164

Jaipur 30
Jaunpur 74, 99,
Kanpur 122
Kazan 105
Kaznin 164
Kerala 107, 113,
Kiev 105
Kora (Jahanabad) 74, 99
Kurnool 113
Lahria Sarai 106
Lucknow 31, 41, 48, 95, 99, 106, 110, 114, 118, 130, 146, 167
Madras 95, 96
Malabar 107, 131, 132
Malwa 54, 55
Mecca 57, 84
Medina 128, 129
Malta 130
Mirzapur 67, 71
Monghyr 107
Moradabad 78, 99, 101, 106
Osmanabad 107
Painam 163
Azimabad (Patna) 67
Pattan 167
Raipur 101
Rampur 78, 93, 94, 106, 117, 118
Rander 70, 107, 109
Saharanpur 101, 104, 105
Samarqand 66
Sarai Mir 110
Sarangpur 55
Shiraz 98, 164
Sirhind 75
Thana Bhawan 101
Thanesar 75, 126
Tonk 42, 77, 118
Trichinopoly 113
Zabeed 164

Notes

1 Panikkar, K. M.: *A Survey of Indian history* (1947), p. 163.
2 Jawaharlal Nehru: *The Discovery of India* (1946), p. 225.
3 Humayun Kabir: *The Indian Heritage* (1955), p. 133.
4 Francois Bernier: *Travels in The Mogul Empire* (1891), pp. 306-7.
5 This Book has recently been published by the Arabic Academy, Damascus, Syria.
6 Gustave Le Bon: *Les Civilisation de L'inde* (Urdu translation by Syed Ali Bilgrami), Book III, p. 146.
7 A crude sort of lamp made of clay, wood or iron, in which mustard oil is generally burnt - Translator.
8 Nehru, Jawaharlal; *The Discovery of India*, p. 218.
9 Abdul Hayy al-Hasani; *Nuzhat al-Khawatir*, vol. IV, p. 345.
10 This book is still unpublished.
11 Sonargaon was the capital of east Bengal during the Muslim rule. It is now known as Painam and forms part of the district of Dacca.
12 A roadside inn where travellers could rest and recover from the day's journey.
13 The individual who undertakes the call to prayer.
14 The person who leads the prayer.
15 An individual who has learnt the whole Quran by heart.
16 Jawaharlal Nehru: *The Discovery of India*, p.219.

17 Hunter, W.W.: *The Indian Musalmans* (1876), pp. 154-155.
18 Reproduced from Sabahuddin Abdul Rahman's *Hindustan ke Ahd-i-Wusta ki ek Jhalak*.
19 Though its name can be translated as *Islamic Culture in India*, this work is actually a literary and educational history of India during the Muslim period. It discusses the evolution of the syllabi, from stage to stage, and also contains an exhaustive list of books written by Muslim scholars on every subject.
20 This was published many years ago by Da'iratul Ma'arif, Hyderabad, and is famous all over the Islamic world.
21 He is known more commonly as Sheikh Ali Muttaqi Gujarati.
22 Imam Suyuti's book is the most exhaustive work on hadith; although, the author has not followed any specific method in the arrangement of the material, the result being that it is exceedingly difficult to consult. If the hadith involves dialogue, it is necessary to know the first few words, and if it is merely narrating an action of the Prophet (s), the name of the narrator is required before it can be found. Sheikh Ali Muttaqi made the treatise more useful and popular by re-arranging it into suitable chapters and sections.
23 Pattan is a town in Gujarat. It is situated about 68 miles to the north-west of Ahmedabad. In the old days, it was called Anhilwarah (and written in Arabic as Naharwalah). In the 11th century, it was the capital of a powerful kingdom of Gujarat when it was conquered by Mahmud Ghazni in 1025. Qutubuddin Aibak reconquered it in 1195.
24 The al-Sihah al-Sittah, the set of six most authoritative works of Hadith: al-Bukhari, Muslim, Abu Dawud, al-Tirmidhi, Ibn-Majah and al-Nasa'i.
25 Al-Fayruzabadi originally hailed from Shiraz in Iran. He was born at Kaznin (Iran) in 1328 CE and died at Zabeed (Yemen) in 1404 CE or 1413 CE.
26 A central-African Islamic state of the medieval era comprising parts of Sudan.
27 This was written under the guidance of the famous scholar and expert of Hadith from Bihar, Maulana Shamsulhaq Dayanawi (who was Maulana Syed Nazir Husayn's favourite pupil). At first, the Maulana himself had begun to write an exhaustive commentary of *Sunan Abi Dawud* under the title of *Ghayat al-Maqsud* but he gave it up after only the first volume had been published. He then had this book written under his supervision and advice by his pupil, Maulana Muhammad Ashraf.
28 Maulana Zaheer Ahsan Shauq was Maulana Abdul Hayy Firangi

Mahali's most worthy pupil. Maulana Anwar Shah Kashmiri used to say of him that a Traditionalist of his stature had not been born in India during the last 300 years.
29 *Tarikh-i-Firoz Shahi*
30 Marshman Clarke: *History of India* (1842) – reproduced on: http://www.ibiblio.org/britishraj/Marshman1/chapter04.html, p. 101.
31 Syed Abdul Hayy: *Mirat-i-Sikandari*
32 Joseph
33 *Nuzhat al-Khawatir*, vol. IV.
34 *Ibid.*, vol. V, p. 217.
35 Carra de Vaux: *Penseur de l'slam* (Paris, 1921).
36 *Tarikh-i-Duwal-o-Azinat* (only the first three volumes of the book in Urdu have so far been published) Composed in two parts of English version, have so far been published.
37 Usman al-Sanad: *Asfa al-Mawarid fi Silsilat Ahwal al-Imam Khalid*, and Muhammad Amin Ibn 'Umar 'Abidin: *Sall al-Husam al-Hindi fi Nusrat Mawlana Khalid Naqshbandi*
38 The first four caliphs of Islam.
39 For a detailed study, see the author's *Sirat Syed Ahmad Shaheed*, Ghulam Rasool Mehr, *Syed Ahmad Shaheed*, and Mohiuddin Ahmad, *Saiyid Ahmad Shahid: His Life and Mission*, published by the Academy of Islamic Research and Publications.
40 Tiqsar
41 Abul Hasan Ali Nadwi, *The Life and Mission of Maulana Mohammad Ilyas*, Academy of Islamic Research and Publications, 1979.
42 Hunter, W.W.: *Indian Musalmans*.
43 Spiritual seminary.
44 The oath taken by a person at the time of becoming the disciple of a saint.
45 Spiritual deputies.
46 The Muslim call to prayer.
47 Abridged from *Tarikh-i-Firoz Shahi* by Ziauddin Barni, p. 346.
48 *Waqa-i-Ahmadi*.
49 *Fawa'id al-Fuwad*, p. 14.
50 *Sirat Syed Shaheed*, p. 249.
51 A Muslim ascetic.
52 Literally' :two *seers*', a *seer* being a measure of weight equivalent to 1.25 kg, although the exact equivalent often varies.
53 *Sayr al-Awliya*, pp. 253-55.

54 *Ibid.*, pp. 271-72.
55 Literally: 'a musical entertainment'. Among the Sufis it is applied to an assembly in which hymns are sung to produce spiritual ecstasy.
56 Same as dervish.
57 *Gul-i-Ra'ana* p. 171.
58 *Nuzhat al-Khawatir*, vol. v.
59 Meaning a *Mansabdar* commanding 3.000 soldiers.
60 Manazir Ahsan Gilani: *Nizam-i-Ta'lim wa Tarbiyat*, vol II, pp. 221-22.
61 *Nizam-i-Ta'lim wa Tarbiyat*, vol. II, p. 220.
62 The word occurring in the original Persian couplet is *faqr*, which means a life of poverty with resignation and contentment.
63 A vessel for holding water.
64 *Siyar al-'Arifin* (Manuscript).
65 *Siyar al-Awliya'*, p. 28.
66 *Ibid*.
67 Meaning relating to the Prophet Ibrahim (Abraham).
68 The call to prayer.
69 The ceremony where the head of the infant is shaved and a sacrificial offering of one or two goats is made to God.
70 Generally, the child is made to recite the first verses ever revealed or a short passage from the first part of the Holy Book. Sweets are also distributed on the occasion.
71 This is the greatest Muslim festival, held on the first day of the month of Shawwal. It is a day of thanksgiving at the successful conclusion of Ramadan, the month in which Muslims are required to fast.
72 A cycle of prayer. A supererogatory prayer is usually made up of two cycles.
73 The second greatest Muslim festival. It is celebrated on the 10th day of the month of Dhu al-Hijjah in commemoration of Abraham offering up his son Ismail.
74 The first chapter of the Quran, offered up for the souls of the dead.
75 The reference is to Hali's poem, *Shikwa-i-Hind*.
76 Ablution performed before prayer.
77 *Ta'am-i-Ishraf* means food one is expecting to come from a particular source.
78 *Ma'asir al-Kiram*, pp. 96-7.
79 *Nuzhat al-Khawatir*, vol. VII, p. 259.
80 *Muntakhab al-Tawarikh*, p. 56.
81 *Tazkira-i-Ulema-e-Hind*, p. 51.

82 *Ma'asir al-Kiram*.
83 *Nuzhat al-Khawatir*, vol. VII.
84 *Ibid*, vol. VI, pp. 243 and 221.
85 *Ibid*., vol. IV, p. 677. The Maulana died after the Sultan in the same year, 1436, or two years later, in 1438.
86 *Aghsan-i-Arba'a*.
87 *Ma'asir al-Kiram*, p. 222
88 Syed Abdul Hayy, *Tarikh-i-Gujarat*.
89 Meaning the course of Islamic theological instruction formulated by Maulana Nizamuddin of Firangi Mahal, Lucknow.
90 This is referring to Jami'a Millia of Delhi.
91 For example, the late Maulana Manazir Ahsan Gilani (Theology), Maulana Abdul Bari Nadwi (Philosophy), Professor Ilyas Bari (Economics), Dr Khalifa Abdul Hakim (Philosophy), Dr Mir Waliuddin (Philosophy), Dr Hamidullah (Politics), Professor Harun Khan Sherwani (Politics), Dr Raziuddin Siddiqui (Mathematics), Dr Mohiuddin Qadri Zor (Urdu) and Dr Syed Abdul Latif (English).
92 A special branch of Islamic literature concerned with the biographies of narrators of the Hadith of the Prophet.
93 For a long time, Dairatul Ma'arif's admirable literary activities continued under the directorship of Maulana Syed Hashim Nadwi and Dr Nizam-uddin. Its present Director is Dr Abdul Moid Khan.
94 *Risala-i-Dairatul Ma'arif*.
95 Paying tribute to the Sultan, Gandhi wrote in *Young India* that he had no peer among those who attained martyrdom in the cause of the country and the nation.
96 Unfortunately, the Sikhs and some of the rulers did not join the popular upsurge, but rather allowed themselves to be used by the British to crush the movement.
97 Azimullah Khan, General Bakht Khan, Maulana Ahmadullah, Maulana Liaquat Ali and Begum Hazrat Mahal were among the foremost leaders of the revolt; Maulana Ahmadullah being the most outstanding. Holmes in his *History of the Indian Mutiny* described Maulana Ahmadullah as: "The most formidable enemy of the British in Northern India." (p. 539). In another of his books, *The Sepoy War*, he paid him the following tribute: "A man fitted both by his spirit and his capacity to support a great cause and to command a great army. This was Abdullah, the Moulvi of Fyzabad." Similarly, Malleson said of him that: "The Moulvi was a true patriot. He had not stained his sword with

assassination. He had connived at no murders: he had fought manfully, honourably and stubbornly in the battlefield against the strangers who had seized his country, and his memory is entitled to the respect of the brave and the true-hearted of all nations." (Vol. IV, p. 381).

98 Admittedly, the Indians too were guilty of gross excesses during this war, like the slaughter of British women and children. However, what the British did by way of retribution can only be described as utter savagery. It certainly did little for the reputation of a people laying claim to culture and civilisation.
99 Munshi Zakaullah: *Uruj-i-Englishia*, vol. II, p. 708.
100 Bosworth Smith: *Life of Lawrence* (1883), vol. II. p. 258.
101 Field Marshall Lord Roberts: *Forty-One Years in India* (1898), p. 142.
102 Reproduced from Ghulam Rasool Mehr (1857).
103 *Uruj-i-Sultanat-i-Englishia*, vol. II, p. 712.
104 Kamaluddin Hyder: *Qaisar al-Tawarikh*, vol. II, p. 454.
105 Edward Thompson, *The Other Side of the Medal*, (1926), p. 40.
106 Adopted from Tufail Ahmed: *Responsible Government and the Solution of the Hindu-Muslim Problem* (1928), p. 56.
107 Details can be obtained from: W.W. Hunter: *The Indian Musalmans* (1876).
108 *Ibid.*, p. 175.
109 *Ibid.*, p. 176.
110 Meaning belonging to the movement for Islamic revival founded by Shaykh Muhammad ibn Abdul Wahhab, an Arabian reformer of the 18th century.
111 Muhammad Jafar Thanesari: *Kala Pani*.
112 *Ibid*.
113 This viewpoint was undoubtedly wrong. It was sponsored by Mr Beck and his successor, Mr Morrison, who for a long time exercised a powerful influence over Muslim politics. The abstention of Muslims from politics during those days proved extremely harmful to them.
114 During his tour abroad, the Maulana succeeded in obtaining letters from the Turkish leaders Enver Pasha and Jamal Pasha promising to support India in its struggle against the British. He managed to send those letters to India concealed in a wooden chest which was packed with silk. This incident became known as the Incident of Silken Letters and has been mentioned as such in the Rowlatt Report.
115 Notable amongst them were Mufti Kifayatullah, Maulana Ahmad Saeed, Maulana Sajjad Behari, Maulana Hifzur Rahman, Maulana

Notes

Ataullah Shah Bukhari and Maulana Habibur Rahman Ludhianwi.
116   The Maulana died in August 1962.
117   *India Wins Freedom* (1958).
118   For example, see the book, *Humare Purwaj*, prescribed for classes VI, VII and VIII in Uttar Pradesh.
119   Article 343.
120   Article 345.
121   The signatures of the children were later excluded from the memorial.

www.ingramcontent.com/pod-product-compliance
Lightning Source LLC
Chambersburg PA
CBHW012005090526
44590CB00026B/3877